# STRANGE ALTARS

# STRANGE ALTARS

## A Scriptural Appraisal of the Lodge

By J. W. ACKER

CONCORDIA PUBLISHING HOUSE · Saint Louis

# STRANGE ALTARS

**P**REFACE: For some years The Lutheran Church — Missouri Synod probably has been the most articulate among the larger Protestant religious bodies in this country in opposition to lodges, especially in its publications. Nevertheless, partly because of the technical nature of the issues involved, the rank and file of the laity of the church has had but a superficial acquaintance with the reasons why the church has refused to admit lodge members to its ranks.

As membership in the principal lodges increased and the number of fraternal orders multiplied, largely because of the prosperity of the last decades, the lay people of our church have been increasingly confronted by lodge members among their friends and business asso-

5

ciates, who have inquired into the reasons why The Lutheran Church — Missouri Synod has objected to membership in fraternal benefit societies. Moreover, pastors of our church body, already overburdened with the pastoral and administrative tasks of their ministry, have been unable to keep themselves fully informed of the latest developments in the area of lodgery.

This combination of circumstances has served to kindle interest during the last years in Synod's lodge position, necessitating much correspondence and many personal appearances at seminars, conferences, and conventions on the part of members of Synod's Commission on Fraternal Organizations.

This monograph is an outgrowth of a series of lectures and essays on the subject of lodgery presented by the author, a member of the Commission. It is not intended as an exhaustive treatment of the subject — nor of any single lodge, but has been prepared as a digest for the purpose of clearly delineating the Scriptural principles underlying the church's stand against the lodge, illustrating as concisely as possible the objectionable features of the fraternal orders considered, treating briefly organizations sometimes erroneously confused with lodges, and spelling out an evangelical, but firm, synodical lodge practice on the basis of the lodge paragraphs of Synod's *Handbook*.

In the preparation of this booklet I wish to acknowledge the debt I owe to the materials accumulated by the late Dr. Theodore Graebner in his pioneering work in this field and to the valuable assistance of Dr. Paul Bretscher, chairman of the Commission on Fraternal Organizations.                    J. W. ACKER

# STRANGE ALTARS

FRATERNALISM, or lodgery, has wielded a not inconsiderable influence in the social, economic, and even political areas of the American scene from the dawn of our country's history. Even in colonial days several secret fraternal benefit societies were transplanted from England and the continent to American soil. Their number multiplied rapidly, and their membership mushroomed in the favorable climate of a democracy. Particularly during that period of United States history when entertainment had not as yet become generally commercialized, individuals and sometimes entire families increasingly sought friendship and amusement within the circle of the lodge, although that type of lodge membership usually increased or declined according to the economic index. Again, political influence and pressure were exerted by some orders, notably Masonry, at various periods of United States history. Finally, certain fraternal groups attracted adherents, especially during the middle decades of the nineteenth century, through their claims to a superior morality and a quasi-religious character.

It was particularly in these last-mentioned spheres that the church, which claimed a monopoly of the religious views and spiritual activities of its members, became concerned about the encroachment of fraternalism upon its private domain. Even the founders of some of the largest Protestant bodies in America expressed hearty disapproval, in instances severe denunciation, of the religious pretensions of certain secret orders. Today conservative religious groups are convinced that any organization which lays claim to the possession of religious truth must be screened and judged by Scriptural standards.

According to that principle it will be our aim to shed Scriptural light on the problem posed for the church by the religious claims and activities of the lodge system. While some seek to dismiss this issue as a sort of "theological scarecrow," we propose to investigate more or less thoroughly the many practical implications of fraternalism, which in many Protestant quarters is little more than a moot question. An intelligent appraisal of the matter should help to clear up some of the misconceptions of lodgery in certain circles and to straighten out some of the fuzzy thinking that at times is ventilated by those who are ill-informed but like to pontificate on this subject.

For that purpose it shall be the avowed aim of this inquiry to avoid all generalizations not grounded on documented facts and to refrain from innuendoes and veiled charges that cannot be supported by quotations from unquestioned authoritative sources. It does not strengthen a position to overstate the case. For that reason all possible objectivity will mark this treatise on fraternalism.

# I. The Problem of the Lodge

## A. A DEFINITION OF LODGE

### 1. Dictionary Definitions of "Lodge"

In order to clarify the issue and avoid confusion in application, it will be helpful at the outset to arrive at a precise definition of a lodge, or fraternal benefit society. According to Webster's Unabridged Dictionary a lodge may be variously defined as "the workshop of a body of freemasons" (obsolete); or "In Masonic and other orders or societies, especially secret societies, the hall or meeting place of a local branch; hence, the body of members composing such a branch." Obviously this dictionary definition is not adequate and therefore not suitable for our purposes. If we shall include all such orders or societies whose chief mark of identification as a lodge would be their secrecy, we should have to include many labor unions, patriotic societies, and fraternal groups in a classification of objectionable organizations. As a matter of fact, although many of our people have thought that the chief objection of the church to a lodge has been its secrecy, this is only a minor consideration. If the church's case against the lodge is to rest principally on the issue of secrecy, the church in any debate on this subject would find itself in a somewhat vulnerable position because of the privacy of some of its own meetings.

## 2. An Adequate Definition for Our Purpose

The real issue lies much deeper and is far more comprehensive and much more involved than secrecy. For that reason we must create a definition of a lodge that will more sharply delineate the features to which we must object because of Scriptural teaching. For our specifically theological purposes we may define a lodge as "a secret fraternal benefit society which has a printed ritual with prayers, altar, chaplain, burial ceremony, an oath, the claim of spiritual advancement, and the guarantee of heaven as a reward for following the principles of the order." Thus the typical lodge in our terminology has the earmarks of a religious system. Nor is this a purely artificial creation, a figment of an overworked imagination. There are numerous organizations which qualify as lodges in this typical sense. As such, though they very likely do not intend to do so, they are in a certain sense in competition with churches. At least to the extent that they seek to satisfy spiritual wants and needs of man and to promote his moral well-being they operate in the same sphere with church organizations. This fact points up the real issue of the lodge as we have defined it. It is its religious element. The religious features and activities of the lodge are the chief concern of the church in its application of Scripture to the life of its members. To this we might add as an object of criticism the worldliness which characterizes so many of the activities of these fraternal societies.

## 3. Illustrations

Illustrations of typical lodges are the Ancient, Free, and Accepted Masons, the Independent Order of Odd Fellows, and the Knights of Pythias. Bearing the characteristic marks of objectionable fraternal societies to a lesser degree are the Benevolent and Protective Order of Elks, the Loyal Order of Moose, and the Fraternal Order of Eagles. These so-called "animal lodges" in their rituals incorporate considerably less of the religious ingredient and, in at least the instances of the Moose and Eagles, have shown a willingness to remove some of the features to which there is objection on the basis of Scripture. The last-mentioned fact will be developed further in a later chapter.

It is obvious that limitations of space will not permit the treatment in detail of all orders which are labeled typical lodges. For that reason we shall confine ourselves to those lodges which more often confront the church in its work.

## 4. Examples of "Lodges" Not Classified as Such

Among the organizations sometimes labeled as "lodges" which are not classified as such because they lack some of the features which characterize the typical lodge are labor unions, railroad brotherhoods, and certain mutual insurance companies, which, while retaining the outward framework of a lodge and an initiation ceremony merely to escape taxation, have for all practical purposes abandoned everything of a religious nature. Instances of such insurance societies are the Court of Honor, the Beavers, the Globe Life Insurance Company, Equitable Reserve Association, and Fidelity Life Association. Orders which, though retaining certain objectionable features, do not make their ritual obligatory or

11

distinguish between fraternal and insurance members are the Danish Brotherhood of America, Daughters of Liberty, Gleaners, Maccabees, etc. Orders which have toned down their rituals, eliminated the altar, chaplain, prayers, oaths, and burial ritual, and which do not in so many words teach salvation by human works, but still retain certain religious traits and objectionable features, such as teaching the universal Fatherhood of God and the universal Brotherhood of man, refer to blind creeds, exalt the charity of the lodge, etc., are the Ben Hur Life Association, Modern Woodmen, and Woodmen of the World.

## B. THE GROWTH OF FRATERNALISM

### 1. The Tendency of Americans to Join Organizations

Americans are known as "joiners." Of all nationalities Americans have the reputation of being the easiest targets for organized membership appeals. So ready, even eager, are many Americans to belong to an organization that they become members merely because the name of a friend or some famous individual is linked with it. Subversive organizations are known to have built their membership lists by the practice of listing on their letterheads the names of successful persons who have carelessly lent their reputations to a supposedly good cause. There is scarcely a human interest or activity for which a society has not been organized. Frequently such organizations have exploited their members for the personal profit of the enterprising founders. And in the general field of social organizations it is almost a physical impossibility to keep pace with the tempo at which societies of virtually limitless objectives are being created, much more to keep fully informed of their many-sided activities.

## 2. The Growth of Fraternal Benefit Societies Encouraged by State Tax Laws

Fraternal benefit societies, or lodges, have shared in the general trend of organizations to multiply and to grow in America today. One of the contributing factors to this mushroomlike growth of lodges in our country during the past century has been the virtually uniform custom of state laws to exempt from taxation all such orders and societies which have a prescribed ritual. A Lutheran lawyer who recently did some research work in this area reported that more than thirty states of the Union follow this procedure. The practice of exempting ritualistic groups from taxation has encouraged the organization of many orders. They have offered a wide variety of insurance and other benefit programs. Frequently they have supported some public charity. But to escape taxation for their financial enterprises, they were compelled to incorporate some form of ritual in their program. This legal requirement accounts for the reluctance of orders having certain typical lodge features to abandon their ritual. Their hesitancy can be more readily understood in the light of this legal technicality.

## 3. National Prosperity a Contributing Factor to This Growth

Another factor in the multiplication and expansion of fraternal societies has been the degree of national prosperity enjoyed by the United States during the last decades. There is an indisputable relation between economic conditions and lodge membership. Prosperity strengthens the lodge system by encouraging the organization of new orders and by enabling established fra-

13

ternities to expand their membership rosters. A period of depression conversely results in the collapse of small, weak lodges and in loss of membership for the stronger orders. Economic and fraternal developments have common resources and move along parallel lines.

# II. Masonry, the Mother of Lodges

## A. A BRIEF HISTORY OF MASONRY

### 1. Legendary Claims to Antiquity

From the general we now proceed to the particular. The mother of the fraternal system is Masonry. The oldest lodge and the pattern for all subsequent orders is the Ancient, Free, and Accepted Masons. The term "Ancient" in its title confronts us with the history of this order. The origins of Freemasonry are obscure because of lack of documentary evidence. We must brand as legendary the claims of modern Freemasons to a great antiquity. Their efforts to project their "peculiar system of morality, veiled in allegory and illustrated by symbols," as far back into time as the days of Noah and the Flood, or to trace the work of the craft to the time of the construction of the Tower of Babel are absurd. Equally fantastic are the legendary references to John the Baptist and St. John the Evangelist as "Christian patrons of Masonry" (Malcolm D. Duncan, *Masonic Ritual and Monitor* [Chicago, 1947], p. 53). The bland assumption that King Solomon of Israel and King Hiram of Tyre were Master Masons together with Hiram Abiff, the architect of Solomon's temple, whose death and resurrection are dramatized in the third, or Master Mason, degree,

14

is entirely without substance in fact. We likewise must dismiss, for lack of evidence, but with somewhat greater respect, the beliefs that were once held in certain quarters of Freemasonry of a historical connection between modern, speculative Masonry and the Dionysian Artificers, the Roman Collegia, or the Comacine Masons. Nor would competent historians acknowledge any historical ties with the Knights Templars. The claim that some of the secrets of the craft had their genesis in the esoteric traditions preserved by stonemasons in Saxon, Norman, or medieval times cannot be substantiated by historical evidence. One even hears such fantastic assertions from the lunatic fringe among the rank and file of Freemasons that our Lord Jesus Himself was a Freemason; that some traditions of the order can be traced back to the Druids, the mysteries of ancient Egypt, or of Eleusis; and that Adam already in the dawn of history was the founder of the order.

## 2. Masonry's Recorded History

In sifting the "wheat from the chaff" we can establish as factual that the term "lodge" was used as early as 1278 to describe the center of activity of stonemasons in those days. "This was a temporary hut or shed put up near the site of the new building which served primarily as workshop, storehouse for tools, the Master's office, and so on. But it seems also to have served as a social center. Masons living away from home would eat and possibly even sleep there; meetings and discussions took place, and a certain fraternal intimacy and fellowship would be established" (Walton Hannah, *Christian by Degrees* [London, 1954], p. 19). In the ancient Masonic constitutions, or old charges of operative masons, there is usually a reference to the Holy Trinity, a series of

15

rules and moral precepts held to be binding on the stonemason, and a brief closing prayer. But scarcely anywhere is there a trace of evidence that a stonemason attached any secret teachings to the practices of his trade or spiritual symbolism to his tools.

Another factor which may have contributed to the development of the Masonic ritual is the Master Mason's word "Mahabone" (sometimes known as Mahabyn, Maughbin, and Machbenach), which originated in Scotland about 1550. Certain ceremonies in the course of time accompanied the imparting of that word. Certain questions and answers were evolved which may have given rise to the Masonic catechizations and lectures of a later area. The Master Mason's word was also imparted with the bodies of the teacher and the neophyte assuming positions in relation to one another as to symbolize the Five Points of Fellowship. These and other usages and customs of operative stonemasons possibly resulted in the development of the speculative element of modern Freemasonry.

It is more difficult to establish clearly how, why, or when the operative stonemason's lodges became purely speculative. In the course of time men who had no connection with the trade became "accepted" members of the craft. The first known instance is that of John Boswell, who in 1600 became an "accepted" member of the Lodge of Edinburgh. By 1670 the "accepted" membership in the Aberden Lodge was in the majority, and by 1717 the "acceptance" group dominated the London lodges to such an extent that they are referred to simply as Freemasons.

Accordingly, the year 1717 marks the birthday of modern Freemasonry. In that year four speculative London lodges met and formed the first Grand Lodge.

The movement was organized, radically altered, and adopted new constitutions. Other lodges joined the movement, new lodges were organized, and Freemasonry spread and prospered. Modern Freemasonry remained on a Christian basis until at least 1723, when in the first edition of Dr. James Anderson's Constitutions almost all traces of Christianity were removed from a previously Christian fraternity as a result of pressure exerted by the prevailing deism and natural (as opposed to revealed) religion of that age of reason (Cf. Walton Hannah, *Christian by Degrees* [London, 1954], p. 26). In 1738 the constitutions were further revised to provide that "Masonry being found in all nations even of divers religions, they are now generally charged to adhere to that religion in which all men agree (leaving each brother to his own particular opinion)." The final apostasy from Christianity, at least in English Masonry, became complete in 1813. On that date under the influence of the Grand Master, the Duke of Sussex, non-Christian universalism and natural religion were established. Only such prayers as omitted Christ's name could henceforth be offered to the Great Architect. In the first charge of the new constitutions only atheists and irreligious libertines were excluded from the lodge, which Rev. J. Fort Newton in *The Builders* (7th ed., 1949), p. 180, describes as "more than a Church . . . not *a* religion but *is* Religion, a worship in which all good men may unite that each may share the faith of all." That remains its position today.

It is difficult to trace the development of the Masonic ritual with any degree of certainty. Semiofficial printed rituals as memory aids for Masonic lecturers did not begin to appear until well into the nineteenth century.

## B. ORGANIZATIONAL STRUCTURE OF MASONRY

A beautifully colored chart with figures published in the October 8, 1956, issue of *Life* magazine illustrates the structure of Freemasonry.

### 1. The Blue Lodge

The Blue Lodge constitutes the foundation of the pyramid that is Freemasonry. The Blue Lodge consists of three degrees, through which every Mason must pass if he is to climb the steps of his lodge. The first degree of the Blue Lodge is the Entered Apprentice degree. The second is called the Fellow Craft degree. The third is the Master Mason degree. Each degree teaches some moral and has certain symbols to represent this moral. The candidate earns the degree by learning the moral lessons and by participating in the ceremonies dramatizing it. Most Masons advance no farther than the Master Mason degree in their lodge work. As Master Masons they are considered to be fully accredited members of the order.

### 2. Scottish Rite

If a Mason wishes to ascend higher into the Masonic hierarchy, he enters either the Scottish or York rites. The Scottish Rite derives its name, according to a popular explanation, from exiled Scottish Jacobites (supporters of the Stuarts after the Revolution of 1688) who in France are supposed to have begun this rite. But the evidence for this theory is very scanty. Be that as it may, since Scotland to a great extent has been the cradle of Freemasonry, the title appears to have been taken as proof of the antiquity and genuineness of these degrees. The Scottish Rite, also known as Ancient and Accepted Rite, consists of thirty degrees, or steps, beyond the Blue Lodge, making a total of 33 degrees. Each of these degrees up to and including the 32d degree is earned. But the 33d degree is honorary and is conferred by the Supreme Council, the ruling body of Scottish Rite Masonry.

### 3. York Rite or American Rite

The other path a Mason may choose in climbing to the higher echelons of Masonry is the York Rite, so called after York, England, where, according to legend, the first Masonic body was organized. It is also sometimes referred to as the American Rite. The York Rite embraces ten degrees, or steps, culminating in the Knight Templar, which is equivalent in rank to the 32d degree, Scottish Rite. Some speak of the York Rite as the Christian path to the top of the pyramid of Freemasonry.

### 4. Side Degrees and Masonic Affiliates

There are several side degrees of Freemasonry:

a. **Tall Cedars of Lebanon of the U. S. A.** This is a side degree with no official standing. It is supposed to bear about the same relation to the Master Mason degree as the Mystic Shrine does to the 32d degree.

b. The **Grotto.** It is officially called Mystic Order of Veiled Prophets of the Enchanted Realm. It is a social organization, bearing the same relation to the Blue Lodge as that borne by the Shrine to the 32d degree and Knights Templars. Its various branches are called grottoes. Its chief objective is entertainment and the enjoyment of carnal pleasures.

c. **Shrine.** Its full title is Ancient Arabic Order of Nobles of the Mystic Shrine. Stevens describes it as "a social and benevolent society with a ritual and history linked to Arabic traditions, in which Oriental mysticism, names, legends, and titles are freely employed." The jewel of the order is the crescent, usually made of the

**19**

claws of the Bengal tiger, united at the bases with a gold setting. The sphinx is engraved on one side and a pyramid, urn, and star on the other. The crescent is generally suspended from a scimitar and holds a star pendant between the drooping horns. Claiming to have originated in Arabia, this order is secret and closely affiliated with Freemasonry. Only 32d-degree Masons and Knights Templars are eligible for membership.

d. **Knights of the Red Cross of Constantine.** This is an order consisting of six degrees, of which three are "working" degrees. Its members must be Royal Arch degree Masons. "The legend is adopted from the story of Zerubbabel and speaks of him and four other Jewish leaders seeking the protection of Darius against the interruptions caused by the Samaritans in the work of rebuilding the temple after the Babylonian Captivity. Having been granted their request by Darius, the latter founded a new order, it is claimed." — *Christian Cynosure,* March 1932, p. 272.

e. **Acacia Fraternity.** This is a Greek-letter fraternity consisting almost exclusively of Masons attending college. Recently its ranks have been opened to non-Masonic students also. Established at the University of Michigan in 1904, it is a sort of club where the brother Masons and friends can be of social benefit to one another. The acacia is an important symbol of third-degree Masonry, standing primarily for the immortality of the soul and secondarily for innocence.

### 5. Affiliated Female Appendages

a. **Order of the Eastern Star.** The Eastern Star is an adoptive rite of Freemasonry. Master Masons only, their wives, widows, mothers, sisters, and daughters are eligible for membership. Organized in 1855 by Robert Morris, the order is made up of subordinate chapters, each of which must have a Master Mason as its "Worthy Patron." The objects of the order are "for a more extended diffusion of the principles of morality and friendship by established and significant emblems, for inciting the influence of females towards the purposes of the Masonic institution; for increasing social enjoyment by the aid of the Masonic tie; for ameliorating the condition of the destitute widow and the helpless orphan; and for affording increased facilities in relieving distressed female travelers." (Robert Macoy, *Adoptive Rite Ritual*, p. 11)

The ritual features five female characters (Jephtha's daughter, Ruth, Esther, Martha, and Electa), who illustrate five moral virtues.

b. **White Shrine of Jerusalem.** This is a social organization of the Eastern Star. According to Masonic authority, it supplies a Christian degree for the deistic Eastern Star. Its ritual is based on Luke 2. Its objectives are fourfold: "Biblical research and further study of sacred history; to unfold and reveal to the initiate a more beautiful understanding of, and devotion to, the sacrificial teachings and example of Jesus of Nazareth; to teach that in the embodiment of faith, love, and good works in our contact with our fellow men and in service to humanity lie the supreme attainments of life; closer friendships that exalt and amplify our conceptions of Christian conduct." Only members of the Eastern Star are eligible.

c. **Order of Amaranth.** Organized in 1653 by Queen Christina of Sweden, it purposes to gather the cream of the Order of the Eastern Star and the Masonic Fraternity into an organization of the highest quality. Another society of similar name was founded by Robert Macoy in

1883. Its ritual is highly regarded in some Masonic quarters. Lectures are offered on Truth, Faith, Wisdom, and Charity. Its work is almost purely benevolent, and its teachings aim at the everyday practice of virtues.

d. **Daughters of the Nile.** This is a secret society of women relatives of Shriners. The branches are called temples and the officers princesses. Its membership is found chiefly in the Western States.

e. **Daughters of Mokanna.** This organization is composed of women relatives of Grotto members. Its subordinate chapters are called caldrons.

### 6. Sponsored Youth Organizations

a. **Order of the Builders.** An order of boys, sponsored and controlled by Master Masons, it includes not only sons of Master Masons between the ages of 13 and 21 but also their closest boyhood companions. Each son of a Master Mason may recommend one friend for membership. The Builders were organized in Chicago.

b. **Order of De Molay.** This is a boys' fraternity organized in 1919 at Kansas City under Masonic sponsorship. The ritual is "built around the fundamental precepts of love for parents, reverence for sacred things, patriotism, purity, courtesy, comradeship, fidelity, and loyalty to the public school as the citadel of American liberty." De Molay was the last Grand Commander of the medieval Knights Templars and died in 1314. Membership in the fraternity is open to boys from 14 to 21 who are sons of Freemasons or vouched for by one of them as a worthy comrade. The organization has a ritual, altar with Bible, chaplain, organist, deacons, burial and memorial ceremony. Its ritual is characterized by deism. The idea of work-righteousness abounds in its pages. "A blameless life robs the grave of its victory" (*Square* *and Compass* magazine, Nov. 15, 1925, p. 48). There are many prayers, but all are Christless.

c. **Job's Daughters.** This order was organized by Masons for female relatives of Master Masons between the ages of 12 and 20 and for other girls who might eventually become members of the Eastern Star. Its heaquarters are at Omaha. National in scope, it seeks "to band together daughters, sisters, nieces, and grand-daughters of Master Masons and of members of the Eastern Star for the betterment of social conditions and to teach practical things." The members are to be impressed with a love of home and country and with a reverence for the Bible. The Book of Job is used for character guidance. There are no prayers in Jesus' name. Salvation is by character. "Righteous service will lead to life eternal." (Ritual, p. 14)

d. **Order of the Rainbow.** Under Masonic sponsorship, this order opens its membership to female relatives between the ages of 12 and 18 of Masons or Eastern Stars, or friends of Rainbow Girls. There is a ritual permeated with deism which speaks of heaven attained by good moral conduct apart from Christ and His atoning work. All prayers omit the name of Jesus. The ritual refers to the Bible as "the rule of right living for all," not the Gospel of Christ's love.

C. MASONRY IN THE LIGHT OF SCRIPTURE

### 1. Masonry Claims to Be a Religious Institution

As a preface to a study of Masonry as a religious institution, which will necessarily result in some critical remarks about the lodge's religion, it should be said in all fairness to the order that it has some excellent and commendable features. For example, Masonry conducts an extensive welfare program. Its charities are widely heralded. Its hospitals, its homes for boys, and the local lodge program of Christmas baskets for the poor are only a few of the better-known services of its expansive system of benevolences. The Grotto supports cerebral palsy clinics. The Tall Cedars of Lebanon raise funds to fight muscular dystrophy. The Shrine maintains seventeen hospitals for crippled children. Moreover, in its ritual the lodge unquestionably encourages and fosters civic righteousness, although its morality is largely shallow, falling considerably short of the Scriptural standards, and in some areas the requirements of acts of charity are limited to brother Masons of the same or superior degrees. Again, the fraternity controls its membership carefully, screening applicants and eliminating undesirables, through a blackball system. In this and other ways Masonry attracts the reputable people of the community.

Despite all this, the church must oppose Masonry because of its religious character. Scripture requires us to pass judgment upon all organizations that enter the domain of religion, ethics, and morality. If Freemasonry falls into one of these categories, we must decide in the light of Bible truth whether a Christian can join this movement.

There are many who will deny that Freemasonry is a religious institution. But for the truth in the matter we must consult the opinion of competent Masonic authority. And on the basis of such qualified opinion Freemasonry must be classified as truly a religious organization. Albert G. Mackey, Past General Grand High Priest and Secretary General of the Supreme Council, 33 degree, for the Southern Jurisdiction of the United States, universally recognized authority on Freemasonry in this

24

country, writes in his *Masonic Ritualist:* "Masonry is a religious institution" (p. 44). On p. 46 he says: "Freemasonry is indebted for its origin to its religious and philosophic character." Again, on p. 14 he declares: "A lodge is said to be opened in the name of God and the Holy Saints John, as a declaration of the sacred and religious purposes of our meeting."

Charles C. Smith in *The Builder,* II, 50, writes: "Masonry is a branch upon the tree of religion. Masonry without religion is like a branch severed from the vine. The particular lodge that is not permeated with the religious spirit is not true to Masonry as such."

In his second volume of *Encyclopedia of Freemasonry,* Dr. Albert G. Mackey has an article on "Religion of Masonry," pp. 617—619. In this article he has this to say: "I contend, without any sort of hesitation, that Masonry is, in every sense of the word, except one, and that its least philosophical, an eminently religious institution . . . that without this religious element it would scarcely be worthy of cultivation by the wise and good. . . . Who can deny that it is eminently a religious institution? . . . But the religion of Masonry is not sectarian. . . . It is not Judaism, though there is nothing in it to offend a Jew; it is not Christianity, but there is nothing in it repugnant to the faith of a Christian. Its religion is that general one of nature and primitive revelation — handed down to us from some ancient and patriarchal priesthood — in which all men may agree and in which no men can differ. It inculcates the practice of virtue, but supplies no scheme of redemption for sin. . . . Masonry, then, is indeed a religious institution; and on this ground mainly, if not alone, should the religious Mason defend it." These quotations sum up

25

what Masonic authorities think of Masonry as a religious institution.

In fact, the front cover page of *The Royal Arch Mason* (Vol. V, No. 9, March 1957), a monthly periodical published by the General Grand Chapter, Royal Arch Masons, carries the following quotation from J. T. Thorp, famous English writer:

## "FREEMASONRY — A SIMPLE RELIGIOUS FAITH"

"We have but one dogma, a belief in God, but this is so firmly established as the principal foundation-stone of the brotherhood that no one can ever be admitted a member of an English-speaking lodge without a full and free acceptance thereof. In all reference to the Deity, God is reverently spoken of as the Great Architect of the Universe. . . . Upon this foundation-stone we construct a simple religious faith — the Fatherhood of God, the Brotherhood of Man, and the Immortality of the Soul — simple, but all-efficient.

"By reason of this simple creed, Freemasonry has been able to attract and accept as members of the Fraternity adherents of every religious faith in the world — Christians, Jews, Hindoos, Mohammedans, Pharisees, Buddhists, and others — atheists alone being excluded. If any member of the fraternity honestly acknowledges his faith in a Supreme Being, whose law is his guide, and to whom he looks for inspiration and guidance in all times of difficulty, danger and doubt, and strives honestly to live by his faith, we care not what the other articles of his creed may be, for we believe that when summoned from this sublunary abode, he will be received into the all-perfect, glorious and celestial lodge above, for he will, by his life, have made of earth the porch-way entrance to Heaven."

After reading this article appearing on the outside front cover of an official magazine of Royal Arch Masonry can anyone still doubt the intent of Masonic authority to teach a "simple religious faith" by their symbolism and dramatization?

Moreover, Masonry has many of the features of a religious institution. The buildings in which Masons meet are called "temples" and "cathedrals." The lodge hall is fitted out with an altar, upon which lies an open Bible. Each lodge has a chaplain, who opens and closes the meetings with prayers, and prefaces initiations and other ceremonies with petitions addressed to a Supreme Being. Speculative Freemasonry is a religious philosophy which pretends to the possession of divine truth. Mackey in his *Masonic Ritualist*, p. 101, writes concerning the ritualistic work of the lodge: "Here must commence his Masonic labor — here he must enter upon those glorious, though difficult, researches, the end of which is to be the possession of divine truth."

The design of Masonic teaching is to point out to its members their relationship to God and mankind and to reveal to them the ultimate destiny of the soul. In the *Iowa Quarterly Bulletin* of April 1917, p. 54, the assertion is made: Masonry is "a divinely appointed institution, designed to draw men nearer to God, to give them a clearer conception of their proper relationship to God as their Heavenly Father, to men as their brethren, and the ultimate destiny of the human soul."

Moreover, Masonry even has a plan of salvation. It distinctly teaches that there is a blessed hereafter, to be reached by all good Masons through the good they do in this life. A Mason is reminded by the lambskin he wears "of that purity of life and conduct which is essentially necessary to his gaining admission into the celestial

27

lodge above where the Supreme Architect of the Universe presides." (Duncan, *Masonic Ritual and Monitor,* p. 50.)

Although Masonry is a religious institution, it is not a Christian institution. Witness its own authorities on this point. Chase in his *Digest of Masonic Law,* p. 208, says: "Blue Masonry (the first three degrees) has nothing whatever to do with the Bible. It is not founded on the Bible. If it were, it would not be Masonry."

Actually, the religion of Masonry is the general religion of nature. It professes to embrace all religions, which it regards as sects. It pretends to select the best features of Christianity, Buddhism, Mohammedanism, etc. It endeavors to become a common denominator for all the world religions, in which representatives of every faith may join on an equal plane. The result is necessarily an anemic, watered-down religious philosophy which has lost its force and meaning in vague generalities.

To demonstrate more clearly that Freemasonry and the Bible contradict each other, we shall quote statements from both. Hearing these conflicting teachings, one can readily see that it is impossible to reconcile Christianity with Freemasonry.

### 2. Masonry's Estimate of the Bible

How does Masonry regard the Bible? Masonry admits a candidate on the basis of his acceptance of the religious source book of his choice. Masonry refuses to prescribe a specific revelation of deity, holding that all religious source books are sufficient guides for faith and life. In effect, the sacred writings of all religions are placed on the same level with the Bible.

Asahel W. Gage in *The Builder,* I, 235, writes: "God's Holy Book, His revelation to us, is the guide in our search for light. To the Jew this Holy Book is the history of Israel, substantially the Old Testament. To the Christian, it is the Old and New Testament. To the Mohammedan, it is the Koran; to the Hindu, the Veda. But whatever book it is, it is the Holy Book of the seeker for Light and that which he believes to be the Word of God. The Holy Book, together with the square and the compasses, are the great lights of Masonry." From this quotation it should be obvious that Gage places the books of revelation of other religions on a par with the Bible. No preference whatsoever is shown.

In the *Iowa Quarterly Bulletin*, July 1915, p. 17, we find this quotation: "Therefore it [Masonry] invites to its altar men of all faiths, knowing that . . . while they read different volumes, they are in fact reading the same vast Book of the Faith of Man as revealed in the struggle and sorrow of the race in its quest of God." Though the Bible is open on the altars of Masonic lodges in this country, that does not mean that it is regarded by them as the only or chief source of revelation. All Masons are reading "the same vast Book of the Faith of Man."

If one as a Christian who believes solely in the authority of the Bible were to insist on the recognition by Masonry of the Bible as the only true Word of God, he would be told substantially what Chase has to say in his *Digest of Masonic Law*, pages 206—208: "To require that a candidate profess a belief in the divine authority of the Bible is a serious innovation in the very body of Masonry. The Jews, the Chinese, the Turks, each reject either the Old or the New Testament, or both, and yet we see no good reason why they should not be made Masons. In fact, Blue Lodge Masonry has nothing whatever to do with the Bible. It is not founded on the Bible. If it were, it would not be Masonry."

In diametrical opposition to such a view of the Bible by Masons we must present the Scriptural teaching that the Bible in all its words is the unbreakable and unalterable Word of God. It is the only divine source of doctrine and rule of life, having the power to save all those who trustfully accept its truths. Here we quote such passages as 2 Tim. 3:16: "All Scripture is given by inspiration of God." 2 Peter 1:20, 21: "Knowing this first, that *no prophecy of the Scripture is of any private interpretation.* For the prophecy came not in old time by the will of man; but *holy men of God spake as they were moved by the Holy Ghost.*" Again, Gal. 1:7-9: *"There be some that trouble you and would pervert the Gospel of Christ.* But though we, or an angel from heaven, preach any other Gospel unto you than that which we have preached unto you, let him be accursed. As we said before, so say I now again, *if any man preach any other Gospel unto you than that ye have received, let him be accursed."* Paul wrote, Rom. 1:16: "I am not ashamed of the *Gospel of Christ, for it is the power of God unto salvation to everyone that believeth."* Jesus said, John 5:39: "Search the Scriptures, for in them ye think ye have eternal life, and they are they which testify of Me."

For further Scriptural testimony on this subject we would refer you to 1 Cor. 2:9-14; Rev. 22:18, 19; John 10:35; 2 Cor. 11:3, 4; 1 Thess. 2:13; Luke 11:28; and 2 Thess. 2:15.

From these and similar Bible passages it should be clear to any intelligent person that a confessing Christian who regards the Bible as God's highest, trustworthy revelation to man, cannot subscribe to the Masonic position that the Bible is only one of many books of equal value in revealing God's will and truth to mankind.

Hence, the Masonic altar for a sincere Christian must be a Strange Altar.

### 3. Masonry's Attitude Toward God

Masonry receives into membership anyone who professes faith in God, regardless of what his concept of deity may be, whether he believes God is a person or merely some force or power. This amounts to the practice of idolatry. In effect, Masonry allows a collection of gods to occupy its altar and thus reduces God to a vague Supreme Being, a nondescript Architect of the Universe, the "Nameless One of a hundred names."

In support of this statement there is this quotation from an article in the *Quarterly Bulletin,* July 1915, p. 17: "Therefore it [Masonry] invites to its altar men of all faiths, knowing that, if they use different names for 'the Nameless One of a hundred names,' they are yet praying to the one God and Father of all."

Ward in *Freemasonry: Its Aims and Ideals,* p. 187, writes: "Freemasonry has taught each man can, by himself, work out his own conception of God and thereby achieve salvation."

In the *New Age,* January 1943, p. 33, we find this quatrain:

> The one Great God looked down and smiled
> And counted each his loving child,
> For Turk and Brahman, Monk and Jew,
> *Had reached Him through the God he knew.*

In a similar vein Albert G. Mackey in his *Lexicon,* in an article on "Religion," p. 404, says: "The religion, then, of Masonry is pure theism on which its different members engraft their own peculiar opinions; but they are not permitted to introduce them into the lodge, or to connect their truth or falsehood with the truth of

31

Masonry." In other words, Masons can hold whatever religious views they will, but they are not permitted to profess them within the confines of the lodge hall.

Again, Newton is quoted in the *Quarterly Bulletin*, January 1917, p. 15, as follows: "While Masonry is theocratic in its faith and philosophy, it does not limit its conception of the Divine, much less upon any one name, for 'the Nameless One of a hundred names.' "

Mackey in *Encyclopedia of Free Masonry*, I, p. 149, writes: "If Masonry were simply a Christian institution, the Jew and Moslem, the Brahman, and the Buddhist could not conscientiously partake of its illumination. But its universality is its boast. In its language citizens of every nation may converse; at its altars men of all religions may kneel; to its creed disciples of every faith may subscribe."

Now, if after reviewing these citations from Masonic authorities a Christian nevertheless feels that he can conscientiously worship the Trinity at the altar of Masonry, he should consider that in the Royal Arch Degree of Masonry the lost Master's Word, for which Mahabone was substituted, is claimed to have been rediscovered after 470 years and is revealed as "Jah-Bul-On." This is the Masonic Trinity. Jah is an abbreviation for the Hebrew name for God, Jahweh, or Jehovah; Bul or Bal is the name for the Assyrian deity; On is the designation for the god of the Egyptians, some contend the God of the sun. In the face of this Masonic concept of God, how can the Christian maintain that he is not guilty of an act of blasphemy if he worships at the altar of Masonry erected to this nonexistent idol? Should not such an altar be for him a Strange Altar?

In short, the Masonic concept of God is deism. Or, more popularly expressed, "Any god will do." Now, if this view of God is permitted to permeate the church and its members are allowed to subscribe to such a notion of God in becoming members of the Masonic fraternity, the church, to be consistent, should abandon all mission work, particularly in foreign fields. Why should we spend millions of dollars in sending missionaries to India, Japan, New Guinea, Africa, etc., and in supporting their work there? Why should we ask young men and women to sacrifice many of the best years of their lives in bringing the Gospel of Christ to pagans, if after all the heathen idol is just another true representation of the "one God and Father of us all," if it makes no difference by what name God is called, so long as you worship Him under some name and by some cult?

If Christian consciences have become dulled by the deism which prevails in our country outside of Christian circles, a review of pertinent Bible passages which denounce such concepts will be in order:

Jesus said: "And this is life eternal, that they might know Thee *the only true God,* and Jesus Christ, whom Thou hast sent" (John 17:3). In Deut. 4:35 we read: "Unto thee it was showed that thou mightest know that *the Lord, He is God; there is none else beside Him."* The prophet Isaiah writes, 44:6: "Thus saith the Lord, the King of Israel, and his Redeemer; the Lord of Hosts: I am *the First,* and I am *the Last;* and *beside Me there is no God."* Our Lord said to Satan at His third temptation: "It is written: Thou shalt worship the Lord, thy God, and *Him only shalt thou serve."* (Matt. 4:10)

Other related passages are, Matt. 28:19; 1 John 5:7; John 5:23; 1 John 2:23; 2 John 9; Ps. 115:4.

From these passages it is evident that Scripture teaches there is only one true God, the Triune God: Father, Son, and Holy Ghost. These three Persons are equal in all things. If one Person is denied or ignored, the entire Godhead is disavowed. All other gods are mere idols.

The Christians of the first three centuries of the New Testament dispensation were aware of this teaching of Scripture concerning the true God and for that reason refused to burn incense and pour out libations at the Roman altars. They had been told that they could add their God to the collection of gods on the Roman altar representing the deities of all faiths. All they were required to do was to acknowledge the gods of other religions on a par with their own. This the Christians refused to do. The Christian faith was, and is exclusive. They said: "Neither is there salvation in any other; for there is none other name under heaven given among men whereby we must be saved" (Acts 4:12). For that conviction they were willing to die. For that attitude toward God they were stretched on the racks, burned at the stakes, thrown to the wild beasts, and made living torches to illuminate the Roman Arena. How many Christians have compromised their faith before the Strange Altars of Masonry!

### 4. Masonry's View of Christ as the Savior of Men

Masonry regards Jesus Christ as a great teacher only, not as the Son of God and Savior from sin, placing Him on the same level with the heathen Greek philosopher Socrates and with the prophet Mohammed. No prayers are ever spoken in Jesus' name in the Blue Lodge (first three degrees), which is the very foundation of Masonry. Only in the 18th and 30th degrees of Scottish Rite Masonry and in the Knight Templar Degree of York Rite Masonry, degrees in which Christianity and its teachings are considered, is it permissible to use the name of Jesus Christ in prayers.

What Masonry thinks of Jesus is exemplified by a quotation from *New Age,* February 1943, p. 100: "Truth planted in the hearts of Socrates and Jesus grew and yielded the fruit of noble lives." According to this article in an official magazine of Freemasonry, Jesus is simply a great teacher whose teachings, like those of Socrates, helped people to lead more noble lives. Nowhere is there any indication that Masonry treats Jesus as the Savior of mankind, whose substitutionary atonement on Calvary wrought forgiveness for all men of all times.

Again, apparently in order not to offend non-Christian Masons the name of Jesus is conveniently deleted from those passages of the Bible prescribed for reading in the ritual because of their value in inculcating certain moral truths, or because of the symbolical implications Masonry has found in them. Thus, for example, in the Royal Arch Degree 2 Thess. 3: 6-16 is read. In this passage Paul admonishes the Thessalonians to withdraw from "every brother that walketh disorderly . . . working not at all, but are busybodies." In verses 6 and 12 the name of Jesus appears. In v. 6 St. Paul says: "Now we command you, brethren, *in the name of our Lord Jesus Christ,*" and in v. 12 he admonishes: "Now them that are such we command and exhort *by our Lord Jesus Christ.*" In both instances the reference to Jesus has been removed from the text, although the section is quoted in its entirety otherwise. The reason is obvious. No one is to be offended by the mention of Jesus Christ as Lord.

The same practice is followed in the Mark Master Degree, where 1 Peter 2: 3-5 is quoted for the opening ceremonies in Mackey, *Masonic Ritualist,* p. 271. This passage has allegorical value for Masonry because Peter refers to Christians as lively stones "built up a spiritual house." The words "by Jesus Christ" in v. 5 are omitted and on the following page Mackey refers to this as a "slight, but necessary modification," although St. Peter asserts that Christians are "to offer up spiritual sacrifices, acceptable to God *by Jesus Christ.*" Our sacrifices cannot possibly be acceptable to God without the atonement of Christ to cover our imperfections.

Again, Mackey, *Masonic Ritualist,* p. 56, says: "The blazing star is said, by Webb, to be 'commemorative of the star which appeared to guide the Wise Men of the East to the place of our Savior's nativity.' This, which is one of the ancient interpretations of the symbol, being considered too sectarian in its character and unsuitable to the universal religion of Masonry, has been omitted since the meeting of the Grand Lecturers at Baltimore, 1842." Need we add any further comment?

Once more, in the Masonic Burial Ritual 1 Cor. 15: 55-57 is quoted. But in v. 57, where St. Paul exults: "But thanks be to God, which giveth us the victory through our Lord Jesus Christ," they put a period after "victory," thus deleting the words "through our Lord Jesus Christ." Certainly the hope of victory over death is hollow and vain without the victory of Jesus over death and the grave that glad Easter morn.

As mentioned previously, the printed ritual prayers for all degrees excepting so-called Christian degrees omit the name of Jesus. Noting this, Christian Masonic chaplains sometimes have inserted the name of Jesus in such prayers. The question whether it is permissible to use the name of Jesus in prayers where the ritual does not provide for such has been decided officially by state Grand Lodges. From the Proceedings of the Grand Lodge of Texas, December 22, 1920, p. 22, we cull this choice bit of information. "30. Questions asked by Secretary, St. John's Lodge, No. 53: 1. Is it un-Masonic for a brother, while praying either in the lodge or at a burial, to close the prayer with the phrase, 'for the sake of Jesus Christ'? Answer: 'No.' "

However, he was overruled by the Grand Lodge, which decreed: "However much it may be regretted, such a question arises in the thirtieth decision of the Grand Master as to the proper conclusion of prayers at burials and in lodges, and while the Grand Master may be right in deciding that it is not un-Masonic, in the sense that charges could not be sustained for such action, in concluding Masonic prayers according to the formula of any religion, still we think that it is contrary to the spirit of Freemasonry and is in derogation of its universality, which would demand that *no phrase or terms should be used in a Masonic service that would arouse sectarian feelings or wound the religious sensibilities of any Freemason.*"

The same position is taken by G. A. Kenderdine in his article "The Idea of God in Masonry" in the *New Age,* pp. 269 ff.: "Masonry has been criticized because its prayers to Deity are 'Christless' prayers. It is improper, in our organization, truly to offer a prayer in the name of Christ or in the name of Buddha or in the name of Mohammed or Allah or any other peculiar and exclusive belief; and when such a prayer is offered, it is simply a violation of Masonic courtesy and propriety. Masonry holds and teaches that with all and above all *there is God, not essentially a Christian Triune God.*"

The *Citrus Mason and Eastern Star,* September 1933, offers this thought concerning Christ: "It is said the essence of Christ's religion is found in the words, 'He went about doing good.' There is enough religion and

37

philosophy in that phrase to save humanity. If each one lived by that rule, his belief or the language of his creed would be immaterial."

But what says the Scripture? The Bible teaches that Jesus Christ is the Son of God, equal to the Father in every respect. He took upon Himself our human nature to redeem a world lost in sin. He alone is the Savior of mankind.

The Apostle John writes, 1 John 5:20: "And we know that the Son of God is come and hath given us an understanding that we may know Him that is true, and we are in Him that is true, even in His Son Jesus Christ. *This is the true God."*

Jesus demands in John 5:23: *"All men should honor the Son even as they honor the Father.* He that honoreth not the Son honoreth not the Father which hath sent Him."

St. John says, 1 John 2:23: "Whosoever denieth the Son, the same hath not the Father; but *he that acknowledgeth the Son hath the Father also."*

John and Peter confessed before the Jewish Sanhedrin: *"Neither is there salvation in any other,* for there is none other name under heaven given among men whereby we must be saved." (Acts 4:12)

Jesus said, John 14:6: "I am the Way, the Truth, and the Life; *no man cometh unto the Father but by Me."*

In Matt. 10:32, 33 we hear our Lord require that we confess Him in the words: "Whosoever therefore shall confess Me before men, him will I confess also before My Father which is in heaven. But *whosoever shall deny Me before men, him will I also deny before My Father which is in heaven."*

Other pertinent Bible passages are John 6:69; 20:28;

1:1, 2, 14; Rom. 9:5; Phil. 2:10-12; 2 John 9; John 10:30; 14:9; Gal. 4:4, 5; Matt. 18:11; John 1:29; 1 John 2:22.

From such declarations of Scripture is it not obvious that a Masonic altar — before which a "Christian Mason" must remain silent concerning his Lord Jesus — is a Strange Altar?

### 5. Masonry's Plan of Salvation

a. Its Teaching of Salvation by Merit

Masonry teaches that heaven is gained by good works. Simply do your best, and the Lord will accept you irrespective of your reliance on Jesus Christ as the Savior of mankind.

In Clymer's *Ancient Mystic Oriental Masonry,* pp. 10 and 11, we read: *"Masonry does not teach salvation by faith, nor the Vicarious Atonement.* Go through its degrees, study the history as taught by its great masters. You can not find that it teaches this doctrine. Boldly I claim that this doctrine (vicarious atonement) does not make Christians, but it does make criminals." It is difficult to conceive of bolder blasphemy than these assertions by this Masonic authority.

From a prayer at "Closing of the Lodge" in Mackey, *Masonic Ritualist,* p. 17, we quote the following: "May we so practice Thy precepts that we may finally obtain Thy promises and find an entrance through the gates into the temple and city of our God."

Again, Mackey in his *Masonic Ritualist,* p. 39, writes: "The Common Gavel is an instrument made use of by operative Masons to break off the corners of rough stones, the better to fit them for the builder's use; but we, as Free and Accepted Masons, are taught to make use of it for the noble and glorious purpose of divesting our hearts and consciences of all the vices and superfluities of life, *thereby fitting our minds, as living stones for that* spiritual building, that *house 'not made with hands, eternal in the heavens.'* "

A quotation from *Minnesota Proceedings,* 1896, p. 47, reads: "How precious the faith possible to every brother as the great change comes before him — 'wrapping the drapery of his couch about him and lying down to peaceful rest'; *'wearing the white rose of a blameless life': calm in the assurance of a blessed immortality.*"

J. Otis Ball in *The Builder,* I, 287, writes: "We find in the Masonic funeral service an allusion to a certain 'pass' whereby we may obtain entrance into the Grand Lodge above. What higher conception could we have of the Master's Word than the pass whereby we can find immortality and entrance into the Grand Lodge on High? *We are told that this pass is the 'pass of a pure and blameless life.'* "

At the close of a Masonic funeral prayer, quoted in Webb, *Freemason's Monitor,* p. 107, we read: "And after our departure hence in peace and in Thy favor, we may be received into Thine everlasting kingdom, to enjoy, in union with the souls of our departed friends, *the just reward of a pious and virtuous life.*"

From the *Quarterly Bulletin,* April 1922, p. 53, comes the following poem:

> The last grand summons has sounded,
> Our brothers have made reply
> And gone to answer the Master
> In that great Lodge on High.
> *Their lives, a pattern perfect,*
> *Whereby to shape our own,*
> *Will be their pass to enter*
> *Before that great white throne.*

When the Entered Apprentice Mason is first presented the Masonic apron, he is expected to explain its symbolism by saying: "Because the lamb, in all ages, has been deemed an emblem of innocence; he, therefore, who wears the lambskin as a badge of a Mason is thereby continually reminded of *that purity of life and conduct which is essentially necessary to his gaining admission into the Celestial Lodge above* where the Supreme Architect of the Universe presides." (Revised Duncan's *Ritual of Freemasonry,* p. 50)

In opposition to such expressions of the hope of salvation by character or good works, Scripture teaches that men are saved solely by the grace of God, through faith in Christ Jesus. Good works, while the necessary fruit of faith, in themselves do not merit our salvation in any manner.

Paul and Silas said to the jailer at Philippi, Acts 16:31: *"Believe on the Lord Jesus Christ, and thou shalt be saved,* and thy house."

Jesus declared: "I am the Way, the Truth and the Life; *no man cometh unto the Father but by Me."* (John 14:6)

Paul wrote, Rom. 3:28: "Therefore we conclude that *a man is justified by faith, without the deeds of the Law."*

Again, he advised the Ephesians, chap. 2:8, 9: "For *by grace are ye saved, through faith;* and that not of yourselves, it is the gift of God; *not of works, lest any man should boast."*

Other applicable Bible passages are Mark 16:16; Gal. 2:16; Col. 1:10; James 2:14, 17; 1 John 1:8, 9; Rom. 3:23, 24; Ps. 14:3; Is. 64:6.

When the assertions of Freemasonry on this point are contrasted with the Bible passages just quoted, an obvious dilemma results. This dilemma which confronts any individual who wishes to be a professing Christian in his church on Sunday, but an honest Mason at his lodge meeting during the week, was recognized by Dr. Elijah A. Coil, a Unitarian pastor in Boston. He prepared a pamphlet entitled "The Relation of the Liberal Churches and the Fraternal Orders," in which he appeals to the consciences of Freemasons by demonstrating their inconsistency in endeavoring to be genuine Christians and true Masons at the same time. On pp. 10 and 11 of his pamphlet he writes:

> That the fundamental difference in the principles embodied in the historic creeds of Christendom and those of our modern secret orders has not been clearly thought out is indicated by the fact that many pledge themselves to both. There are lodge men who, in the churches, subscribe to the doctrine that "We are accounted righteous before God only for the merit of our Lord and Savior, Jesus Christ, by faith and not for our own works or deservings," and enthusiastically assent to the following declaration: "Although our thoughts, words and actions may be hidden from the eyes of men, yet that All-Seeing Eye whom the sun, moon and stars obey, and under whose watchful care even comets perform their stupendous revolutions, pervades the inmost recesses of the human heart, and will reward us according to our merits."

> A little child, once its attention is called to the matter, ought to be able to see that it is impossible to harmonize the creed statement here quoted, with the declaration taken from the monitor of one of our greatest and most effective secret orders, and found in substance in the liturgies of nearly all the others. If "we are accounted righteous before God, only for the merit of our Lord and Savior, Jesus Christ, by faith and not for our own works or deservings," then it can not possibly be true that the All-Seeing Eye "pervades the inmost recesses of the human heart, and will reward us according to our merits." One of these declarations excludes the other. *Men can not*

42

*consistently subscribe to both. They do, however, subscribe to both, and are thereby led into inconsistencies which they do not discern.*

Dr. Coil then appeals to lodge members to be consistent and join his Unitarian church, where they can profess the same truths they do in the lodge. For a Christian an altar which in effect symbolizes salvation by character instead of Christ is a Strange Altar.

b. Masonry's Claims that All Faithful Masons
   Reach Heaven

Masonry implies that all its members who are faithful to the principles it inculcates will reach the Grand Lodge above. Witness this quotation from Mackey's *Masonic Ritualist,* p. 238: " (Freemasons) *mutually promote* the welfare and happiness of each other to the honor and glory of God and *the salvation of our own souls.*"

An excerpt from the *Minnesota Proceedings,* 1895, p. 66, reads: "He who approaches our altar in good faith and by the light which we bring him receives our teachings into a heart already prepared and lives a life in conformity with the principles which he here imbues, has come into an invaluable possession and need have no fear when the word shall come calling him into the hereafter but that *he will be received as a living stone fit for that temple not made with hands.*"

Another quotation from the *Minnesota Proceedings,* 1896, Appendix, p. 17, reads: "These beloved brethren have laid down their working tools. Their work was done and well done. *They have been transmitted from the fading honors of an earthly Lodge to* the enjoyment, we can confidently hope, of *an inheritance 'incorruptible, undefiled, and that fadeth not away.'* "

The above perversion of a well-known Scripture passage, combined with other quotations from bona fide

43

Masonic sources, will suffice to illustrate the fact that Freemasonry pretends that all of its faithful members will reach "that temple not made with hands" in heaven, entirely apart from faith in the atoning blood of Christ. Of such a scheme of salvation, called universalism, Scripture knows positively nothing. Rather our Lord said: *"He that believeth and is baptized shall be saved.* But he that believeth not shall be damned" (Mark 16:16). Also compare Rom. 3:28 and Eph. 2:8,9; Acts 16:31 and John 14:6, quoted elsewhere in this treatise. Masonry's altar is a Strange Altar also in this respect.

### 6. Masonry's Unionistic Practices

In the Masonic lodge hall people of all faiths meet and worship together. Here Christian, Jew, Mohammedan, Hindu, and Buddhist can join in common prayer to gods of any description and preference. Under the vague label "Supreme Architect of the Universe" or the nondescript designation "the Nameless One of a hundred names" they can worship on a common footing, each acknowledging his own, but none daring to confess his specific deity, lest he offend the sensibilities of one of a different faith. This practice of worshiping in an atmosphere of vagueness and in a spirit of "agreeing to disagree" is repugnant to the Christian who has been trained to confess his Savior and not to compromise the truth of His Word.

Scripture forbids the joint worship of those not united in the same faith. Paul warns, Rom. 16:17: "Now I beseech you, brethren, mark them which cause divisions and offenses contrary to the doctrine which ye have learned, *and avoid them."* Obviously the apostle here insists that Christians dare not worship with those who are not one in faith with them.

The same apostle writes 2 Cor. 6:14-18: "Be ye not

44

unequally yoked together with unbelievers. For what fellowship hath righteousness with unrighteousness? And what communion hath light with darkness? And what concord hath Christ with Belial? Or what part hath he that believeth with an infidel? And what agreement hath the temple of God with idols? For ye are the temple of the living God, as God hath said: I will dwell in them, and walk in them; and I will be their God, and they shall be My people. Wherefore *come out from among them, and be ye separate, saith the Lord,* and touch not the unclean thing; and I will receive you and will be a Father unto you, and ye shall be My sons and daughters, saith the Lord Almighty." If anything is clear from this lengthy passage, it is that Christians are forbidden to worship with non-Christians. Christians are righteous before God through the perfect righteousness of Christ, which covers their sins and imperfections. Therefore they can have no spiritual fellowship with those who are unrighteous before God in the filthy rags of their own merits. Christians are spiritual light. Therefore they can have no communion with the spiritual darkness of unbelief, even in the Masonic Lodge, which is guilty of a major deception when it promises to bring the neophyte to the "light." Such unionistic worship, which is so distasteful to God, is again a strange altar for the sincere and conscientious believer.

### 7. Masonry's Blasphemous Oaths

Masonry requires of all candidates for each degree that they obligate themselves in advance to safeguard the particular secrets of each degree, including its characteristic password, grip, duegard, and secret teachings at all costs, binding them with an oath which calls upon God to keep them "steadfast in the due performance of the same" under the dire threat of the most hideous penalties. This procedure for all practical purposes amounts to blasphemy of the Most High God.

We shall quote only the penalties for the first three degrees (Blue Lodge) of Freemasonry.

At the First or Entered Apprentice degree the candidate obligates himself: "Binding myself under a no less penalty than that of having my throat cut across, my tongue torn out by its roots, and buried in the rough sands of the sea at low water mark, where the tide ebbs and flows twice in twenty-four hours, should I ever knowingly or willingly violate this my solemn oath and obligation as an Entered Apprentice Mason. So help me God, and keep me steadfast in the due performance of the same."

The wording of the oaths for the second and third degrees of Blue Lodge Masonry are the same as the First, with the exception of the penalty. The penalty at the Second, or Fellow Craft, degree is: Having my left breast torn open, my heart plucked out, and given as a prey to the wild beasts of the field and the fowls of the air."

At the third, or Master Mason, degree the penalty exacted of the candidate is: "Having my body severed in twain, my bowels taken from thence and burned to ashes, the ashes scattered to the four winds of heaven, so that no more trace or remembrance may be had of so vile and perjured wretch as I."

Scripture forbids using the name of God when not necessary or in uncertain matters. Particularly, it should wound the sensibilities of the faithful Christian to be called upon to employ the name of God to the accompaniment of hideous penalties to help him preserve the comparatively trivial secrets of Masonry.

In this connection Ex. 20:7 comes to mind: "Thou

46

shalt not take the name of the Lord, thy God, in vain; for the Lord will not hold him guiltless that taketh His name in vain."

Our Savior in His comments on the Second Commandment in His Sermon on the Mount, said, Matt. 5: 34-37: "But I say unto you, Swear not at all; neither by heaven, for it is God's throne; nor by the earth, for it is His footstool; neither by Jerusalem, for it is the city of the Great King. Neither shalt thou swear by thy head, because thou canst not make one hair white or black. *But let your communication be yea, yea; nay nay; for whatsoever is more than these cometh of evil."*

St. James writes in his epistle, chap. 5: 12: "But above all things, my brethren, swear not, neither by heaven, neither by the earth, neither by any other oath; but *let your yea be yea, and your nay, nay, lest ye fall into condemnation."*

Altars before which such hideous, blasphemous oaths are taken surely are Strange Altars for the true Christian.

This somewhat thorough discussion of the false religion of Freemasonry will serve to point up the errors of the religion of fraternalism in general. The religion of the lodge is the natural religion of the Fatherhood of God, the brotherhood of man, and the immortality of the soul. Moreover, it is an anemic, watered-down version at that. Masonry's religion has become the pattern for the religious philosophy of all other lodges. In fact, prominent Masons have almost without exception prepared the rituals of the lesser fraternities. So intimate are the ties between the larger orders that lurking in the background there seems to be a virtual interlocking directorate in this secret empire. Words, entire phrases, and allegorical passages of the Masonic ritual are reproduced, perhaps subconsciously, in the rituals of practically all

47

other lodges. It is for that reason that the identical false doctrines of Masonry are found ingeniously interwoven into the texture of such rituals, although not in so coarse or offensive a manner, as a rule. In the rituals of some lodges, particularly recently revised rituals, the parent influence of Freemasonry has become quite remote, and offensive expressions are less frequently found. But, generally speaking, the principal features of Freemasonry will be found more or less clearly stated in the rituals of the lodges to which we shall next address ourselves. It will therefore be necessary merely to illustrate these principles from the rituals of the respective lodges. In order to avoid unnecessary repetition, the Scripture passages that refute the characteristic teachings of the lodge will be omitted. They can easily be located by referring to the section on Freemasonry under which they were cited.

## III. The So-called "Animal" Lodges

A. THE EAGLES (FOE)

### 1. Brief History

The Fraternal Order of Eagles was founded at Seattle, Wash., in 1898, by a group of "Bohemians," mainly for purposes of pleasure. It once was known as a bartenders' union.

Its principles are Liberty, Truth, Justice, and Equality, and it professes the "Golden Rule laid down by Christ." The branches of the order are called "aeries."

The Eagles were organized as a fraternal benefit society, but since 1927 no longer sell insurance. About one half of the members continue to pay for sick benefit, which amounts to only one dollar a day for a number of weeks. The death-benefit clause of $150 to $300 is optional.

Most of the members today join because of social reasons. Among their charitable projects the Eagles for many years sponsored relief for flood disaster, but with the frequent recurrence and magnitude of these disasters the order has been compelled to curtail this program.

The fraternity since 1949 has operated the Eagles' Home in Berlin-Spandau conjointly with CARE. The lodge prevailed upon the British occupational authorities not to demolish this 500-year-old building and is now using it for a carpenter-training school for some 400 German boys ranging in age from 14 to 18.

The headquarters of the fraternity now is Milwaukee. Judge Robert Hansen, a former Missouri Synod Lutheran, now is chairman of the Board of Trustees. Its membership is 750,000. Insurance benefits paid since its organization total more than 127 million.

## 2. Evaluation of Ritual

The Fraternal Order of Eagles, judged by its ritual, is a lodge in the synodical sense of the term.

The Eagles are a secret society. The initiate is asked to take an oath not to reveal the secrets of the order.

The lodge room is fitted with an altar, upon which lies an open Bible. The candidate must profess a belief in deity, not necessarily the Triune God. This stamps the order, which inculcates "the universal Fatherhood of God" and "the universal brotherhood of man" (Ritual., p. 76) as a religious society.

There is a chaplain who opens and closes meetings and prefaces certain ceremonies with prayers, which are uniformly Christless in order not to offend the non-Christian.

The lodge has a burial ritual, which, however, is optional. By implication, all members faithful to the principles of the fraternity are admitted to "the Grand Aerie" above.

From the Funeral Ceremony there is this quotation to support that statement: "He who lies here was both friend and brother. Knowing that he believed in the eternal principles of this Order, we are comforted. He valued liberty, loved Truth, and was just in his dealing with all men, and gracious and brotherly in all the observance of true equality. He believed in the existence of a Supreme Being, the Father of us all, Giver of every good and perfect gift, and in this belief he died, in the hope of a blessed immortality beyond the grave. He bore the trials of life and fought its battles till, tired and weary of the struggle, he fell asleep. *For him eternal rest remains.*" (The Rituals of the FOE, p. 68)

Nevertheless there have been some recent developments, which will be pointed out in another section of this book, which indicate that the officials of this order are willing to remove as many of the objectional features of the ritual as they can without going before the convention of the fraternity for ratification. It is feared that it would be difficult to gain the consent of the rank and file to radical changes.

## B. THE ELKS (BPOE)

### 1. Brief History

The Benevolent and Protective Order of Elks was organized in New York City in 1868. At first the fraternity was known as "The Jolly Corks," either from the flying corks that came from bottles or because their membership was largely drawn from the theatrical profession. The name "Elk" was finally adopted. The founders of the order were chiefly Freemasons, as is evidenced by the use of aprons in Elk ceremonials and certain features of the ritual familiar to workmen of the quarries.

The fraternity was "designed to contribute to the social enjoyment of its members, to relieve the necessities of deserving brethren, their widows and orphans, and to perpetuate the memories of deceased members of the Order." The eleventh hour of the night is the mystic hour of the order, consecrated to the memory of the dead.

The lodge has enjoyed a rapid growth and now numbers 1,750 lodges, with a membership of 1,149,613. Its headquarters are in Chicago. L. A. Donaldson is the Grand Secretary.

### 2. Evaluation of Ritual

The Elks are a typical lodge as defined previously. They are a secret, oath-bound society. The obligation the candidate takes is offensive. At initiation he says: "I _____, in the presence of God and this lodge of Elks, do solemnly promise and swear that I will never reveal any of the confidential matters of this Order. . . . I will never knowingly violate the chastity of any pure woman [sic]. If I break this oath, may I wander through the world forsaken; may I be pointed out as a being bereft of decency and manhood, too loathesome to hold communion with true and upright men."

The ritual has religious features: Bible on altar, chaplain, prayers, oath on the Bible, a way of life which stresses the virtues of fidelity, charity, justice, and brotherly love.

The fraternity is a deistic organization. God is not defined, though the candidate is expected to express his belief in God. God is referred to in the prayers as "Our Father Who Art in Heaven," "Almighty God whose Fatherhood of man makes all men brothers," "Exalted Ruler of the Universe," etc.

All the prayers are Christless. However, in the prayer spoken in the ceremony "Announcing the Death of a Brother" there is a vague allusion to "Thy redeeming grace and power," which some Christian member of the Eagles might construe to refer to Christ's merits for sinners. Nevertheless, there is no mention of Jesus' atonement for sinners anywhere in the ritual.

Salvation by merit (character) is inculcated by the ritual in various places. A sample is found in the memorial service, where the treasurer says, p. 6: "To teach my brothers that when their earthly accounts are closed, *it will be their deeds on earth which will aid them in partaking of the treasures of the better world.*" Note also the ceremony for "Announcing the Death of a Brother," which expresses sentiments like this: "He has passed into the light which is beyond the valley of the shadow of death."

### 3. Social Membership

Although the officials of the Elks insist there is no sanctioned social membership in the Elks Fraternity, known as Elks Club or otherwise, there is abundant evidence that locally many lodges provide for such social memberships, by which those who do not wish to become obligated under the ritual may enjoy the social facilities of an Elks lodge by paying an annual fee which varies from place to place.

## C. THE MOOSE (LOOM)

### 1. Brief History

The Loyal Order of Moose was organized at Louisville in 1888 by three members of the Knights of Pythias who were theatrical performers. It is an international social and benefit fraternity "always ready to join hands in uplifting and advancing the cause of humanity." For nineteen years the order barely survived. In 1906 James J. Davis, Secretary of Labor in President Harding's adminstration, joined as the 247th member. He had remarkable organizational ability, which caused the fraternity to expand rapidly.

Its membership is open to white men, of sound mind and body, good standing in the community, engaged in lawful business, and able to speak and write English.

Although originally conceived with three degrees for strictly ritualistic purposes, the lodge in recent years has become so engrossed in the promotion of Mooseheart that its ritual has been greatly simplified. It is not strictly an insurance society, although there are small weekly benefits and a nominal funeral payment.

The principal objective of the order is to advance Mooseheart. In the preamble of their constitution (*Constitution and General Laws* [in effect as of October 1, 1949]) we read: "The objects and purposes of said fraternal and charitable lodges . . . are to unite in the bonds of fraternity, benevolence, and charity. . . ."

Its social objectives are "the development of manhood along the lines of Moose ideals of Purity, Aid, and Progress."

The order, which is active in the United States and possessions, Canada, and the British Isles, operates Mooseheart, a school and home for boys and girls of deceased members, and Moosehaven at Orange Park, Fla., a home for aged dependent members and their wives. Headquarters are at Mooseheart, Ill. Paul F. Schmitz is Director General. Membership totals 1,063,708. Benefits paid total more than 73 million dollars.

### 2. Evaluation of Ritual

While the LOOM is still a lodge in a modified sense, it has recently made a number of notable changes in its ritual which renders it less objectionable. Nevertheless it still contains considerable religiously offensive material.

In the Initiatory Ceremony, which is the only ritual most Moose have seen or heard, the candidate takes an obligation from which the word "swear" has been removed and "promise" substituted. However, the pledge is administered with left hand on the heart and the right hand raised. In his response to the obligation, the candidate cannot help but feel that he is taking an oath.

Much of the secret element has been removed from the ritual, although there still is a solemn promise not to reveal "any information — concerning anything — I may hereafter — hear, see or experience — in this Lodge."

There is only one prayer in the Initiatory Ceremony, p. 18, and it is Christless.

A number of offensive expressions have been stricken

54

from the ritual, such as the reference to "vain dogmas," p. 11; "as the Mohammedan turns toward Mecca; nor faith, nor creed, nor dogma will deny," p. 17, for which was substituted "with bowed heads, and none will deny"; and "oath" on p. 19 was stricken in favor of "obligation"; also, "and listening, love can hear the rustle of a wing," borrowed from Robert Ingersoll, and others of lesser significance.

Although much of the religious content of the ritual has now been removed, there still is an altar with an open Bible lying on it present in the lodge hall. An obligation still somewhat in the nature of an oath is required. The references to God still have a deistic flavor. A Christless prayer remains. Accordingly, the LOOM still retains some of the elements of a lodge as defined herein.

# IV. Recent Developments in Lodgery

## A. GENERAL OBSERVATIONS

### 1. Multiplication of Fraternal Societies

As observed in the introduction to this study, in late years, particularly in the last generation, there has been a tremendous mushrooming of fraternal societies. The general high level of prosperity in our country has been a major contributing factor of this growth. Of such multiplication there seemingly is no end. This situation will likely continue as long as the people of our country are eager to join any organization that captures their interest.

## 2. General Decline of Ritualism

At the same time that fraternalism is expanding, there is a noticeable general decline of interest in ritualism. Particularly men's lodges are experiencing considerable difficulty in enforcing the ritual. Almost without exception officials of an order insist that the ritual be kept strictly in force, but at the local lodge level the officers find it increasingly difficult to enlist and train drill teams to dramatize the ritual. This is not necessarily true of women's organizations, however. Women's groups seemingly have a predilection for pomp and ceremony.

## B. Meetings of Commission with Lodge Leaders

### 1. National Grange

Beginning with April 9, 1943, your commission has held five meetings with officials of the National Grange, including both the present National Master, Herschel Newson, and his predecessor in office, Mr. A. S. Goss, now deceased. Two of these meetings were held at the Hotel Lincoln in Indianapolis, one at Concordia Seminary, St. Louis, another at Hotel Statler in St. Louis, and the last at the Conrad Hilton Hotel in Chicago, January 21, 1955.

These meetings were candid and yet friendly. A better general understanding was reached between the Grange and our church. Both National Masters of the Grange were very co-operative and desirous of removing the objectional features we found in the Grange ritual. But because of the reluctance of the Order of Demeter, which is the group in charge of the ritual, to make any changes in this seemingly sacrosanct document of the Grange that has gone virtually unchanged in 80 years, little of a tangible nature was accomplished. Mr. Newsom has invited our commission to meet with him to explore further possibilities.

## 2. Veterans of Foreign Wars

Representatives of our commission have met twice with VFW officials, the first time April 21, 1944, at St. Paul, the second time April 13, 1951, at VFW headquarters in Kansas City, Mo. The second meeting was particularly fruitful. At this meeting Adjutant General R. B. Handy agreed to drop the oath hitherto required of candidates in obligating them to the ritual of this order in favor of a promise. As a result of agreements reached at this meeting, it is now possible to become a member of the VFW merely by signing an application card with a printed form of obligation that does not require the candidate to be initiated under the ritual.

## 3. Moose

As a result of four meetings held with officials of the LOOM between April 1951 and April 1956, the ritual of the LOOM has been revised to eliminate a number of objectionable features, described in detail in the evaluation of this order's ritual.

## 4. Elks

Since December 1953, three meetings have been held with representatives of the BPOE. These meetings were always friendly and pleasant. For a time it appeared that officials of the order would yield to our representations. However, these hopes were dashed when, in a letter from James R. Nicholson, General Manager of the

BPOE, in May 1956, we were informed "that the Advisory Committee of the Order did not deem it advisable to make any changes in the Ritual." The situation remains unchanged since.

### 5. Eagles

A more encouraging report can be given of the developments that resulted from four meetings held with leaders of the FOE since January 11, 1952. Progress was noted at that first meeting at their headquarters, then in Kansas City. Throughout the meetings that followed, the officials of this order were extremely cooperative and eager to meet our objections. Finally their officials offered our commission an alternate initiation ceremony which was unobjectionable. The difficulties attending the implementation of this alternate initiation, however, caused the College of Presidents at their meeting on February 5, 1958, to postpone final approval of the alternate initiation ceremony and to agree to study this document in the light of all its implications with their respective District Vice-Presidents for another year before reporting back to the February 1959 meeting of the College of District Presidents. For the present, then, we are marking time in our efforts to eliminate the objectionable features of this lodge.

### 6. Odd Fellows

At the invitation of the IOOF our commission met with their officials in the Fontanelle Hotel, Omaha, September 14, 1956. This meeting was productive only of the information that their ritual had been greatly improved by revision and in a better understanding of our mutual positions. Nonetheless the Odd Fellows are still classified as a lodge.

# V. The Attitude of Christian Churches Toward Lodges

## A. NON-LUTHERAN CHURCHES

### 1. The Roman Catholic Church

In checking with the office of the Archdiocese of St. Louis periodically, our commission has learned that the Catholic Church's attitude toward lodges remains absolutely unchanged. The Roman Catholic Church in this country deals with the problem of fraternalism by canon law. When a question is asked of Catholic officials as to what the church's stand is regarding lodges, they immediately quote Canon Law by number. This applies not only to Freemasonry but also the lesser lodges. However, the Catholic Church does not view the so-called "Animal Lodges" with alarm, but assumes a tolerant attitude over against them. In fact, opposition to these orders is relaxed if there is any prospect of infiltrating them and of controlling their program from within. In that manner the church can eliminate whatever proves to be objectionable.

### 2. Eastern Orthodox Churches

In the last several years the Orthodox bodies in our country have become increasingly aware of the menace of Masonry and have noticeably stiffened their opposition to this fraternity. From the book *The Orthodox Church Militant,* by Eusebius Alexander P'Stephanou, published recently in New York, the following is said concerning the attitude of the Greek Orthodox Church toward fraternalism: "Masonry trespasses the bounds of the Church by interfering with ethical and religious truths. The very fact that Masonry deals with religion and worship makes it mandatory for the Orthodox to avoid Masonry and all lodges and organizations of a similar character. Religion and ethics is the business of the Church. To insist that one can be an Orthodox in good standing and a Mason at the same time is simply to betray a gross ignorance of the mission and nature of Christ's Church."

The same applies to the Russian Orthodox Church in this country. Recently a resolution was approved by the Ninth All-American Church *Sobor,* which specified, among other things, regarding Masonry: "That any Orthodox Catholic Christian, whether he be a bishop, priest, deacon, or layman, loses all the rights, honors, and privileges of his membership and of his office in the Church when he joins any esoteric, syncretic, or secretive organization."

Regardless of whether this resolution is enforced or not, there is a noticeable strengthening of the opposition of the Eastern Orthodox bodies to fraternalism in this country today.

### 3. Protestant

Although the founders of the Protestant churches were almost unanimous in their opposition to Masonry, their successors in the large Protestant denominations have not been so vocal in their witness against the evil of fraternalism, with the result that there is practically no objection to membership in the Masonic Order, certainly not in the lesser orders, within the ranks of the greater Protestant bodies today. There are, of course, in practically all the prominent Protestant church bodies minority or splinter groups which make an issue of lodge membership. But by and large Protestantism is quiescent in its opposition to lodgery. One of the notable exceptions, of course, is the Christian Reformed Church.

## B. LUTHERAN CHURCHES

### 1. Other Lutheran Bodies

Your commission recently conducted a survey of the attitudes of all Lutheran bodies toward lodgery. The results, incorporated in a tract the commission published under the title of "Lutheranism and Lodgery," reveal that in theory and principle, that is, in terms of synodical resolutions and official pronouncements, practically all Lutheran bodies in our country disapprove of lodge membership. But, in many instances such resolutions and pronouncements condemning the evil of lodgery are for all intents and purposes a dead letter. Nothing is said or done to enforce the resolutions. In fact, in some areas the lodge is regarded as no problem whatever, and solicitation for lodge membership among members of Lutheran congregations is tolerated. This results in an embarrassing situation whenever Lutheran union is under discussion.

### 2. Synodical Conference Synods

There is complete harmony in principle, if not in practice, among the bodies constituting the Synodical Conference. Any deviation from opposition to the lodge in these circles is confined to individual congregations in certain localities, where laxity on the part of some pastor caused a lodge problem to develop.

### 3. Practice of The Lutheran Church — Missouri Synod

The practice of our own church body is clearly defined in its constitution. From time to time, problems arising in the interpretation and application of the constitutional paragraphs are considered at synodical conventions, and measures are taken to attain a greater uniformity in practice. It may be stated that in general, despite the rapid expansion of fraternalism in our country, the lodge practice of the Missouri Synod remains firm and even gives indication of becoming more functional.


# VI. A Recommended Policy in Dealing with Lodge Members

### A. HISTORICAL DEVELOPMENT OF A POLICY

From the first decades of its history The Lutheran Church — Missouri Synod has regarded lodge membership a barrier to reception into the fellowship of the church. From time to time it reaffirmed its position toward secret orders. The general policy was that no one affiliated with a lodge could become, or remain, a communicant or voting member of our congregations. Already at an early date it became customary to insert a "lodge paragraph" into the constitutions of congregations. This served as a testimony against the lodge for the benefit of those who were received into the congregation, as well as a safeguard for the congregation and as a guarantee to Synod of soundly Scriptural practice. Beginning with 1849, articles on fraternalism appeared at regular intervals in the official periodicals of our church.

In 1873 the Eastern District went on record as permitting the communing of lodge members for a limited time, but with such stringent restrictions as to reduce the cases to a minimum.

Finally in 1926 a committee was appointed to formulate something approaching an official synodical policy regarding lodges. Its report, adopted at the synodical convention in 1929, resulted in the formulation of the paragraphs on "Synod's Position Concerning Lodges" in the synodical *Handbook*. From time to time these have been revised to meet new situations and problems as they arose.

Over a period of many years the sainted Dr. Theo. Graebner, long-time professor at Concordia Seminary, St. Louis, and editor of the *Lutheran Witness,* as a personal hobby gathered detailed information about fraternalism that served to undergird Synod's position concerning lodges. His files of such materials grew to voluminous proportions, and since his death have been turned over to Synod.

In the twenties a Bureau of Information was created to provide information and advice on lodge matters. In 1950 its name was changed to "Commission on Fraternal Organizations," which is a truer description of its function. At the 1956 synodical convention its membership was increased from three to five. One seminary professor, one pastor, one teacher, and two laymen serve on the commission. The commission is obligated by the constitution of Synod to "furnish information, advice, and literature concerning lodges" and to "prepare and disseminate periodic reports" on changes that have taken place in the various lodges.

B. Current Policy

### 1. Synodical Constitution Paragraphs

Synod's position concerning lodges is stated in 14.03 of the synodical *Handbook*. In par. *a* Synod declares that it is firmly opposed to lodges. In par. *b* every pastor is obliged to instruct his people on the "sinfulness of such lodges." In par. *c* fellow Christians, fellow pastors, and especially the officials of Synod are required to admonish in the spirit of Matthew 18 a pastor who neglects this duty. In par. *d* officers, pastors, and congregations are urged "to admonish such congregations and pastors as permit the 'lodge evil' to exist in their churches without countertestimony and decisive action." In par. *e* the various Districts are asked to "carry out these provisions and faithfully to assist their congregations in eradicating the 'lodge evil.'"

Since paragraphs *f* and *g* were radically changed at the St. Paul Convention of Synod in 1956, we quote them here in full:

f. It is, and shall be, the practice of the congregations of Synod not to administer Holy Communion to members of such lodges, nor to admit such persons to communicant membership, since Holy Communion expresses an exclusive spiritual relationship of the communicant to his Lord and to his brethren. (Matt. 10:32; 1 Cor. 10:16, 17; and 1 Cor. 11:25)

g. (1). A pastor will sometimes encounter exceptional cases in which he is called upon to administer Holy Communion to a person who is still outwardly connected with such a lodge.

(2). Such exceptional cases, however, are normally limited to those instances in which the individual involved has renounced, to his pastor and/or the church council, the unchristian or anti-Christian teaching of the lodge of which he is a member. In such cases the pastor shall consult with his brethren in the ministry or with officials of Synod, as the case may require.

(3). Furthermore, in such exceptional cases the pastor should earnestly beware of procrastination and of giving offense, both to the members of the congregation and to brethren in general.

(4). Finally, the pastor should put forth continuous

64

effort to bring the individual to an early decision in this matter so that he may be fully won for Christ and become or remain a communicant member of the congregation, as the case may be.

## 2. Outline of Policy

On paper it may appear simple to interpret and to apply the provisions of the lodge paragraphs of Synod's constitution. In practice, however, many difficulties arise. For that reason an outline of synodical policy in dealing with varying conditions is provided here.

### a. Different Kinds of Orders

In former days the task of dealing with a lodge man was comparatively simple. Practically all lodges were deistic, pagan, and anti-Christian. It was not too difficult to produce the evidence from the lodge rituals. Every member was received through initiation, and at the initiation he was bound to the ritual. That made it comparatively easy to reach the conscience of the lodge man and to convince him that he should sever his connection with the order.

Today, however, the situation is entirely different. There are many lodges which have changed their character in recent years. *Some lodges have abandoned their lodge character entirely* and have reorganized themselves into mutual insurance societies or civic clubs. They eliminate everything of a religious character — the altar, the chaplain, the prayers, the oaths, the burial services, etc. In order to classify as a fraternal benefit society and to escape taxation as an old-line insurance company, they retained the framework of a lodge with a simplified initiation ceremony of some kind. Such are the Fidelity Life Association (formerly Mystic Workers of the World), Mutual Legal Reserve Life Insurance (formerly Court of Honor), National Mutual Benefit (formerly The Beavers), *et al.*

Certain lodges *have eliminated much that was objectionable from their rituals,* but they still have a few religious references. It would therefore be unfair to classify them as typical lodges.

Some secret orders *have retained their ritual,* at least officially, *but in practice the ritual has been permitted to fall into disuse.* Members pay their dues to a treasurer or secretary, and that is all there is to it. Such are: The Modern Woodmen, Woodmen of the World, and others.

Some lodges *have retained their ritual, but have made it optional for the local.* In some communities the ritual is used, in others it has not been used for years. Somewhat similar are the orders which have retained the ritual but have made it a rule to omit the ritual upon the objection of any member, or provide that attendance at ritual meetings is optional. Such are: Ancient Order of United Workmen of North Dakota and Montana, United Commercial Travelers, *et al.*

Some lodges *have retained the ritual but recognize our objection to syncretistic worship.* For those who object to fraternalism they provide that they may send their application for insurance to the main office and pay their premiums to the main office. They are not obligated or initiated and not considered members of the local. This amounts to a clear-cut distinction between fraternal and beneficiary members. Judged by the ritual, they are a lodge. However, they maintain a separate insurance department for such as refuse to join the lodge. Examples: Degree of Honor, Ben Hur Life Association, Maccabees.

Some lodges have retained their ritual. However,

66

they *provide an alternate initiation* which does not obligate to the ritual those who do not wish to be initiated under the ritual: Example: Eagles, Independent Order of Foresters.

b. Different Kinds of "Lodge Members"

As today there are various types of lodges, so there are differing types of lodge members:

1) Members (of regular lodges) *who actually participate* in idolatrous and/or unionistic worship, i. e., worship involving those not agreed in belief.

2) Members (of regular lodges) who are initiated and bound by the ritual, but *no longer attend meetings.*

3) Members who attend the meetings and participate in the work of *societies which have eliminated many objectionable features,* such as oath, prayer, etc., but still retain certain objectionable features.

4) Members who were initiated and obligated, but who *no longer attend meetings, and* who *expressly repudiate the teachings and practices of their lodge,* desiring merely to retain their insurance and avoid losing what they have paid in.

5) Members of *societies which* retain certain objectionable features but *make the ritual optional* for the local and for the individual applicant and are willing to excuse members from all responsibility for the ritual and practice of the lodge. These members should voice their objection to the ritual and make it clear that they desire to be classed only as beneficiary or insurance members.

6) Members of *unobjectionable orders.*

c. Attitude of the Church

Current policy is our church acknowledges that there are differences in lodges and different kinds of lodge members. These distinctions require careful discernment and faithful, intelligent treatment by pastors and congregations.

Those who participate in idolatrous and/or unionistic worship should, after loving instruction has proved fruitless, be suspended from Holy Communion and be disciplined and eventually excommunicated from the congregation.

Those who are members of a typical lodge but do not themselves participate in the worship of the lodge are subject to church discipline. Synod has left the question of temporarily communing such members as have renounced the religious features of the lodge to the judgment of the individual pastor, who is to consult with his church council, conference brethren, and Visitor.

It is also current policy to recognize the existence of borderline lodges which have eliminated the usual lodge features, oaths, Christless prayers, salvation by works, burial ritual, etc., but still have some objectionable religious references — or which, while retaining certain objectionable features, make the use of the ritual optional or distinguish between fraternal and beneficiary members. Such instances become cases each of which must be determined on the basis of its individual circumstances.

Resolutions of Synod recognize that there are cases of casuistry concerning which there can be justifiable differences of opinion because of the interplay of complicating factors. In such instances the pastor should consult with his conference brethren and synodical officials.

d. An Evangelical but Firm Practice

In dealing with such different types of lodge members of varying types of lodges, the faithful pastor should not operate with the lodge paragraph of his congregational constitution, nor with the resolutions of Synod regarding lodges. He should not threaten the individual by saying: "You can't be a member of my church," or: "You will at once be excommunicated." Nor does he use moral coercion by asking "What would your sainted father or mother say if they knew that you had joined a lodge?" Again, the evangelical pastor does not immediately suspend from Holy Communion without offering proper explanation.

But in every instance the faithful pastor's approach to the lodge man must be dictated by a love for the soul of the individual lodge man, "for whom Christ died." Believing in the power of the Word, the evangelical pastor by instruction from Scripture, specifically the doctrines of the Trinity and the way of salvation solely by the merits of Christ, gives the Holy Spirit a chance to work. He will point out to the lodge man the Christless prayers in the ritual, the unnecessary oaths, the oaths in uncertain things, the blasphemy of Masonic oaths, the universalism of the lodge (i. e., all members of the lodge will be saved), the moral idealism and humanism in the rituals (i. e., man not the subject of God), the unionistic forms of worship (compromising the truth), and the difference between natural and revealed religion. He will point out the glory of being a member of the church, which is the body of Christ, and will demonstrate the inconsistency of being a member of a religious order which does not acknowledge his Head, Jesus Christ. The evangelical pastor will stress a few simple, basic points and drive them home. He will not overwhelm the lodge member with a flood of theological terminology with which he is not familiar.

If after such instruction the lodge member persists in participating in the idolatrous and syncretistic worship of the lodge, he must be further dealt with and finally disciplined. But the member's degree of knowledge, intelligence, and attitude will determine the manner and the length of time of dealing with him.

*Members of typical lodges who have ceased to attend meetings* and to participate in the ritual, must nevertheless be dealt with. They must be shown how inconsistent it is to belong to the church of Christ and to an anti-Christian order at the same time. They must be made to feel that they share some responsibility for the teachings of the lodge, even though they do not attend the meetings. By their membership they may give offense to weak members who will follow their example and join the lodge. Whether the evangelical pastor will commune such a member while the negotiations are going on depends on the individual as well as on local conditions. The board or the council of the congregation should always be kept informed. Finally, if the lodge man will not listen to brotherly admonition, he must be excommunicated from the church. It is impossible to say how long one must continue to deal with such a person before excommunicating him. The lodge in question, the attitude of the individual, and local conditions must determine that.

*Members of borderline lodges,* though they cannot be charged with idolatry or syncretistic worship, must nevertheless be dealt with and must be shown they have joined a society which teaches false doctrine or indulges in practices contrary to the Word of God. If they defend those teachings and practices, continue to participate in the unionism of the lodge, praise the "charity" of the lodge to the disparagement of the work of the church, and in other ways show that they have imbibed the fraternalism of the lodge, they are subject to discipline.

*Members of borderline orders which make the ritual optional* and absolve members having conscientious scruples, and in some cases all applicants, from initiation and hence from responsibility for the ritual or practices of the lodge — members who have availed themselves of this provision or concession and who promise to testify against the evils they may encounter in the lodge, cannot be disciplined as lodge members. Under these conditions they have only a business connection through their benefit or life-insurance contract or social association. However, there still remains the possibility of offense to weak members who are not acquainted with the circumstances.

The evangelical pastor will instruct his members regarding lodgery in catechetical classes, society meetings, voters' assemblies, etc. He will not inveigh in general terms against the lodge from the pulpit, although occasional sermons devoted to a full treatment of a certain lodge or Scriptural objections to the lodge system may be in order in some instances.

# VII. Miscellaneous Organizations

### A. CIVIC CLUBS

The civic clubs, businessmen's clubs, athletic associations, and the like which are an accepted segment of our modern community life are not be be classified as lodges. In fact, the civic clubs in their constitutions omit any reference to religion and often forbid the discussion of religion at their meeting places. The only trace of religion at their gatherings may be a table prayer. They are listed here merely for purposes of clarification.

### 1. Kiwanis

Founded in Detroit in 1915, the Kiwanis Club International is an artificial Indian name. The membership consists of business and professional men who are officers, partners, or chief executives of their firms, and each local club is limited to two from each line of business.

Kiwanis was organized for the practical application of the principle of the Golden Rule to modern everyday life. The organization seeks to convert smug, self-satisfied professional and businessmen into ardent and unselfish workers for benevolent and charitable purposes, such as child welfare. It is the hope of Kiwanis that tired business and professional men may become radiant personalities of contagious good cheer and fellowship.

Religion has no place in the official program of the association. Membership, 251,000 (1957).

### 2. Rotary

Rotary International was founded in Chicago in 1905 by four men who adopted the name Rotary because they met in rotation at their respective business offices.

From the official publication *What Is Rotary?* is drawn the following statement of objectives of this business club:

"The Rotary Club is organized to express the proper relation between private interests and . . . society. To accomplish this purpose more effectively, the principle of limited membership has been adopted, the Rotary Club consisting of one representative from each distinct line of business or profession.

"The Rotary Club demands fair dealings, honest methods, and high standards in business.

"Service is the basis of all business.

"He profits most who serves best."

Membership, 450,000 (1957).

### 3. Lions

Founded in 1918, the International Association of Lions Clubs is a civic club of the noonday-luncheon type like the Kiwanians and Rotarians. The name Lions is an abbreviation of the slogan "Liberty and Intelligence: Our Nation's Safety."

Its objects are: "To promote the theory and practice of the principles of good government and good citizenship; to take an active interest in the civic, commercial, social, and moral welfare of the community; to unite the members in the bonds of friendship, good-fellowship, and mutual understanding; to provide a forum for the full and free discussion of all matters of public interest, partisan politics and sectarian religion alone excepted; to encourage efficiency and promote high ethical standards in business and professions, provided that no club shall hold out as one of its objects financial benefits to its members." Membership, 566,000 (1957).

The Kiwanian, Rotarian, and Lions clubs are not lodges or secret societies. They are businessmen's or commercial clubs existing for the purpose of advancing good business ethics and relations and for engaging in community service.

### 4. YMCA

The Young Men's Christian Association was founded in England in 1844. The "Paris Basis" test of membership of 1855 specified: "The Young Men's Christian

Association seeks to unite those young men who, regarding Jesus Christ as their God and Savior . . . desire to be His disciples in their doctrine and in their life and to associate their efforts for the extension of His Kingdom among young men."

The "Evangelical Test" of membership adopted at Detroit in 1868 was more stringent, limiting membership to applicants who are "members in good standing of an evangelical church." Those churches were considered evangelical which, "maintaining the Holy Scriptures to be the infallible rule of faith and practice, do believe in the Lord Jesus Christ (the only-begotten of the Father, King of kings, and Lord of lords, in whom dwelleth the fulness of God bodily, and who was made sin for us, though knowing no sin, bearing our sins in His own body on the tree) as the only name under heaven given among men whereby we must be saved from everlasting punishment and to life eternal."

However, there is a tendency toward liberalizing the membership restrictions and toward greater vagueness of the "C" in YMCA, for in 1925 it was resolved to admit to membership and to committees of local branches, Catholics and Jews, not to exceed ten per cent of the local membership.

The student associations have long ago abandoned the evangelical test of membership, except as to officers. Nor is church membership any longer required.

On the basis of this creed (for that it is in effect), the YMCA unites into a religious fellowship for worship and religious work those who subscribe to its religious tenets. Since it arbitrarily selects only certain Christian teachings as essential for fellowship, it is a unionistic organization. Today the religious work of the YMCA is thoroughly saturated with Modernism.

But the YMCA does distinguish between active members, who have the right to vote and hold office, and associate members, who pay for the club features, educational and athletic privileges, without becoming active members. The organization does not demand a religious pledge or confession from those who simply desire to use the facilities of its colleges, business and vocational schools, gymnasiums, reading rooms, etc. Hence it cannot be maintained that by paying fees for such services a person necessarily enters into spiritual union with the YMCA as such. Also, holding a position in the educational program, athletic departments, or libraries could not be labeled a denial of faith.

## 5. YWCA

Organized in England in 1855 and transplanted to the United States in 1858, the Young Women's Christian Association has as its professed aim the moral, social, and intellectual well-being of young women. Its members are banded together to encourage thrift and purity and to afford help in sickness. The means employed are evening classes, reading rooms, gymnasiums, holiday homes, circulating libraries, saving funds, bureaus for securing positions, and aid to travelers. Instruction is offered in religious knowledge through Bible classes and in common worship, but attendance is not a condition of membership nor morally obligatory. They are merely offered as "opportunities for improvement."

There is no restriction of membership on the basis of a religious test, although formerly it insisted on church membership as a condition of membership.

Although the YWCA deserves much credit for caring for transient and working girls, the word "Christian" in its name can scarcely be justified by such human-

75

itarian activity. It is fundamentally a unionistic and anti-confessional organization.

As in the case of the YMCA, memberships only for the use of reading rooms, pools, gymnasiums, libraries, and employment agencies of the YWCA are not to be considered approval of the religious position of this organization.


## B. VETERANS ORGANIZATIONS

Veterans organizations have played a prominent role in the history of our country. As their membership increases with the present policy of compulsory military service, their influence will also likely grow.

### 1. American Legion

The American Legion is a patriotic organization of men and women who did service for the United States. Its chief purpose is the cultivation of "one hundred per cent Americanism."

A committee of The Lutheran Church — Missouri Synod met with American Legion committees in 1919 and 1921. Through these contacts certain lodge features which were about to be included in the ritual were eliminated. In place of a ritual a "ceremonial" was adopted. Prayer at post meetings is permitted by majority vote. But because of pressure brought to bear by our men a note is usually appended to each ceremonial, to wit: "In case such member of the Post objects on conscientious grounds to prayer being offered, it shall be omitted, and in its stead the members shall stand in silence for thirty seconds, provided the same is so ordered by the majority of the members present."

At the time of its organization the America Legion made use of the ritual optional. Nevertheless it will be necessary for our pastors to remind our Legionnaires to exercise their privilege to protest against prayer in meetings in order to avoid engaging in unionistic practices. Some posts of the Legion have dropped the ritual altogether.

A "Short Form of Initiation Ceremony," which is entirely unobjectionable, is provided for in the Manual. It has no religious features. The Ceremonial is introduced by the statement: "In order that every new member may receive some form of initiation where it is not practical to conduct the full initiation ceremonies, the following short form has been authorized so that all new members may take the obligation and receive a proper introduction to the American Legion."

This statement permits us to tell our Lutheran applicants that if they wish to join the Legion, they should insist on being initiated on this short form.

Our pastors should also warn their veterans who belong to the Legion not to participate in social activities of the Legion that conflict with the Christian way of life.

### 2. Veterans of Foreign Wars

According to its constitution, the purposes of the VFW are:

> "The purposes of this corporation shall be fraternal, patriotic, historical, and educational: to preserve and strengthen comradeship among its members; to assist worthy comrades; to perpetuate the memory and history of our dead, and to assist their widows and orphans; to maintain true allegiance to the Government of the U. S. A. and fidelity to its constitution and laws; to foster true patriotism; to maintain and extend the institutions of American freedom; and to preserve and defend the U. S. from all her enemies, whomsoever."

Accordingly, the VFW is not designed to build character, to cultivate spiritual life, or to prepare for the life to come. In the constitution there is no religious reference, except mention of services to be performed by the chaplain.

However, the ritual has a strong religious flavor. It contains prayers and a complete burial service. In the prayers there is no mention of Jesus Christ. God is addressed as "Lord of battles," "Commander of the universe," "Captain of our salvation," etc. The Bible is referred to as follows: "In it you will find the precepts of true comradeship and citizenship, to which we all aspire." It is just a Book of the Law, no Gospel. The burial service contains a number of references to eternal life and exhortations to live a life which will make the living "worthy" to enter heaven.

Despite all this, it should be said that the ritual is not strictly of the lodge type, since it contains no ethical or religious teachings, no principles for life. It is also common knowledge that in some posts the ritual has been dropped and that members are not always obligated to take part in memorial services.

It should also be noted that Section 110 of the amended Bylaws of 1946 reads: "Provided the accepted applicant has subscribed to the membership obligation, he shall be considered a member in good standing as soon as elected and be so notified by the Post Quartermaster, who shall mail or deliver to the new member the official regulation dues receipt for the current membership term.

"The conferring of membership by oral obligation shall not be obligatory. All members elected as heretofore prescribed shall be members in good standing with

78

the same privileges as though they had taken the ceremonial obligation prescribed by the Ritual of the VFW of the U. S."

From this it follows that membership in the VFW on this basis, as with the American Legion, does not conflict with the principles of our church. Compare also the comments regarding the VFW under IV-B-2.

### 3. Disabled American Veterans of the World War

The DAV is "a National Organization of and for all wounded, injured, or disabled men and women who served in the World War." Its ritual contains an opening and closing prayer, and a benediction. There is no pledge to secrecy. The chaplain's prayer in the burial service is objectionable because it assumes that every DAV is finally saved.

However, the use of the burial service and appointment of a chaplain is optional with each chapter. Each state department and local chapter may adopt its own rules and regulations. Also, each camp may decide by majority vote whether prayer shall be used or omitted.

For these reasons the DAV may be classified with the American Legion and VFW for our purposes here.

### 4. American Veterans of World War II

The AMVETS were organized in Kansas City in 1944. Any American citizen is eligible for membership in this organization who was "regularly enlisted, inducted, or commissioned" in the Armed Forces of the United States or our allies on or after September 16, 1940, and who served between that date and the cessation of hostilities, provided that he was honorably discharged.

The objectives of the AMVETS are as follows:

"To uphold and defend the Constitution of the U. S. A.; to safeguard the principles of freedom, liberty, and justice for all; to promote the cause of eternal peace and good will among nations; to maintain inviolate the freedom of our country; to preserve the fundamentals of Democracy and Americanism; to perpetuate the friendships and associations of the Great War of Liberation, and to dedicate ourselves to the cause of mutual assistance."

There is a chaplain who opens and closes meetings with prayer. There is no secret ritual. Very little is provided in the way of rites. There is a ceremony for semi-military funerals.

Apparently these considerations classify the AMVETS aside of the veterans organizations previously mentioned.


## C. FRATERNITIES AND SORORITIES

Although our commission has written for information of interest to us to all fraternities and sororities and has carried on correspondence with 34 of these, we have the rituals of only three of them and the constitutions or pledge books of eleven others. All social fraternities are members of The National Interfraternity Conference. The individual societies are held to keep their rituals absolutely secret.

In general, classified by their type of membership, there are two kinds of fraternities and sororities: (1) those whose membership is not restricted to men or women who have attended college; (2) those who admit only college-going young people or alumni.

The first group is almost entirely social in character, although there are several organized to pursue educational and cultural objectives. The organizations which

80

do not have attendance at a college or university as a test for membership are made up almost exclusively of sororities. As a rule, men are not attracted by this type of organization, but will join some lodge instead, or engage in athletic, social, educational, and cultural activities outside such groups.

The college fraternities and sororities, in turn, may be subdivided into social, professional, and honorary. The professional and honorary fraternities almost without exception have no religious elements in their rituals, if they happen to have one. In that regard the college social fraternities are entirely different. Practically all of them have rituals. Generally these rituals are available only to the officers, sometimes only to the president, of the chapter. The meetings are secret. Prayers, usually Christless, are spoken at the opening and close of meetings, and for special functions. In the rituals and pledge books of the college social fraternities and sororities which we have examined we have usually found objectionable material, such as expressions reflecting natural religion, self-righteousness, and snobbery. The prayers usually involve the members in unionistic practices. The obligations to secrecy usually take the form of oaths. Also, in some instances the moral reputation, particularly of men's groups, leaves much to be desired. A general atmosphere of worldliness envelops the social fraternity system at our colleges and universities. Since not a few of our college-going Lutheran youth will desire to join such social fraternities or sororities, our pastors and parents should discuss with them the character of the organization which is rushing them, warn them against those which may endanger their faith, and urge those who have pledged themselves to questionable organizations to withdraw.

### D. LABOR UNIONS

Since the closed shop is becoming an increasingly important issue in industry today, many laboring people of Christian congregations must belong to a union to hold a job. Since all labor unions are secret and their character sometimes resembles that of a secret order, we occasionally are confronted by a difficulty in congregational practice in dealing with members of such organizations.

Those which have religious ceremonies and exercises, prayers, and religious teachings (like those of the lodges) must be judged, of course, on the basis of these objectionable features. At the same time we must recognize the different character of unions as such. They are labor organizations, not created for purposes of brotherhood along fraternal but along industrial lines. Religion is not the essence of labor unions. Religious principles and teachings are not their declared purpose. Hence we cannot deal with union members as we would deal with lodge members.

By this we do not wish to say that we would assume an attitude of absolute toleration. Even industrial organizations may impose conditions impossible for Christians to accept. Whether such is the case with the individual union depends upon the character of its ritual and its activities.

Undoubtedly there are cases where withdrawal from the union might become a condition of continued communicant membership, as, e. g., violence in labor disputes, "goon" tactics in strikes, or any other unlawful practices sponsored occasionally by irresponsible men. But in that case the principles of the Moral Law would apply, not the principles governing fraternalism.

Where the union has a ritual, the question must be raised whether it is in actual use. If so, is the union member obligated to participate in the prayers? If there is a burial ritual, does it contain elements of work-righteousness and universalism, and if so, is the union member compelled to participate?

It should be obvious that the affiliation of our members with labor unions is in each case a matter of casuistry.

### E. Youth Organizations

#### 1. Boy Scouts

The Boy Scouts of America are a secular organization with a program of work and play for boys. It is international in scope. Boys between eleven and fourteen are eligible for membership. The movement strives to train these boys in resourcefulness, personal self-control, thrift, courage, loyalty, and other virtues that make for efficient manhood and good citizenship.

Article II of the Constitution states: "The purpose of this corporation shall be to promote, through organization and co-operation with other agencies, the ability of boys to do things for themselves and others, to train them in Scoutcraft, and to teach them patriotism, courage, self-reliance, and kindred virtues, using the methods which are now in common use by Boy Scouts," namely, by emphasizing the Scout Oath or Promise and the Scout Law for character development, citizenship training, and physical fitness.

The Scout Oath or Promise reads:

> On my honor I will do my best —
> To do my duty to God and my country,
>     and to obey the Scout Law;

83

> To help other people at all times;
> To keep myself physically strong, mentally awake,
> and morally straight.

The Scout Law specifies twelve points as follows:

> A Scout is trustworthy, loyal, helpful, friendly,
> courteous, kind, obedient, cheerful, thrifty,
> brave, clean, and reverent.

In the explanation of these points under the Scout Law in the constitution, specifically religious implications are found only in the development of points (3) — "A Scout is helpful," and (12) — "A Scout is reverent."

Under point 3 is found the controversial Good Turn, concerning which the Scout Law says: "He must do at least one Good Turn to somebody every day." Admittedly, without the proper guidance this statement of Scout Law could foster pharisaical self-righteousness and encourage the belief that an eternal reward awaits him who abounds in such good works.

Concerning the point 12 that "A Scout is reverent," the Scout Law says: "He is reverent toward God. He is faithful in his religious duties, and respects the conviction of others in matters of custom and religion." Without the proper interpretation this statement could easily promote deism.

Concerning the need for the Scout Oath or Promise and the Scout Law to provide motivation for this program, Article IV of the Constitution regarding Principles has this to say:

> The Boy Scouts of America maintains that no boy can grow into the best kind of citizenship without recognizing his obligation to God. In the first part of the Boy Scout's Oath or Promise, the boy declares, "On my honor I will do my best to do my duty to God and my country, and to obey the Scout Law." The recognition of God as the

84

ruling and leading power in the universe and the grateful acknowledgment of His favors and blessings are necessary to the best type of citizenship. . . . The Boy Scouts of America therefore recognizes the religious element in the training of the boy. . . . Its policy is that the organization or institution with which the Boy Scout is connected shall give definite attention to his religious life.

In further exposition of this attitude, Elbert Fretwell, Chief Scout Executive, sets forth the relation of the Boy Scouts to the church in the following terms:

We recognize that there is no Boy Scout authority which supersedes the authority of the local pastor and the congregation in any phase of the program affecting the spiritual welfare of Lutheran men and boys in Scouting, and the purpose of this Lutheran Manual (Lutheran Committee on Scouting) is to guide the pastor and congregation in their efforts to supplement the Scout Program with the spiritual program of the Church.

Furthermore, Dr. Ray O. Wyland, Director of Education, speaking for the National Council, in a letter of June 2, 1932, elaborated on the relationship between Scouting and the church further as follows:

The Organization (B. S. A.) makes no attempt to direct the religious or moral training of the boys in Church troops. . . . "A Scout is reverent": This affirms a true Scout's obligation to observe the right of other people to have their religious convictions. . . . The National Council will keep the channels open to representatives of the Church and will welcome comment, criticism, and suggestions leading to the discovery and elimination of inconsistencies between the stated policies and the printed word in its official publications. These same policies must also govern the Local Councils of the Movement.

He stated that control by the Scout movement "refers to the physical and mental accomplishments only, the religious guidance being entirely under the control of the Troop Committee."

Moreover, he explained that whatever Scouting as such has to say about religion refers to "civil righteousness" — termed "character building and citizenship training," "good citizenship through service."

Regarding the Scout Oath he said: "The Boy Scout 'Pledge' is a promise, not an oath in the Scriptural sense of the term. The upraised hand, with three fingers extended, has reference to the threefold pledge, not to the Trinity."

Even a Lutheran boy who is a member of a community troop may appeal to his congregation for a decision against a sectarian Scoutmaster, according to Dr. Wyland: "In Churches too small to sponsor troops or where the boys of the congregation affiliate with community troops, the Church shall govern their activities according to Lutheran policies."

There is nothing wrong about the Scout Promise and Scout Law, provided it is properly motivated, he explains: "According to Lutheran teaching, fulfillment of the Scout Promise and the Scout Law is God-pleasing so long as motivation, means, and end remain in keeping with Scripture."

There was a time, of course, early in the history of the Boy Scout movement, when the organization sponsored instruction that had definite "religious values" and "spiritual ends" in view as an achievement of the Scout program. As a rule this turned out to be naturalistic doctrine, reflecting the Masonic philosophy of the English founder of the organization, Sir Robert Baden-Powell. It was he who in 1908 conceived the idea of the Boy Scout movement. The Scout program was brought to the U. S. by W. D. Boyce of Chicago in 1909. It was incorporated in our country in 1910. In 1916 the BSA was granted a Federal Charter by Congress.

In the earlier days absolute control over the spiritual motivation for the Scout program of church troops was not vested in the congregation or congregational Scout troop. It was provided, indeed, that "parent institutions administer their own troop." But while the parent institution (congregation) was called "the source of power," it did not possess the authority that was later vested in it through a revision of administration at the local level. Earlier congregational troop committees served only as an advisory committee to the Scoutmaster. Now the troop committee secures the Scoutmaster and serves as his supervisory committee. In effecting this change of policy, Dr. Wyland wrote December 12, 1925: "We have tried to make every necessary provision to insure that the local Lutheran church will have both supervision and direction of the Scout program with its own boys under its own leadership."

Accordingly Synod's Board for Young People's Work in 1930 after a thorough study approved of the Scout program of physical and educational activities, declaring: "Standards of proficiency have been established for these various activities, and merit badges are awarded as progressive degrees of ability are achieved."

Regarding the objections previously raised against the Scout program, the Board reported:

1. "After discussing at considerable length the objections to the oath, we conclude that the promise is not an oath in the Scriptural sense of the term."

2. Regarding the objection to the "good turn" they concluded: "A Lutheran troop is under Lutheran control and religious instruction and must be taught to view the 'good turn' in its proper light."

3. The Board declared that the danger of unionistic worship is not inherent in the movement, but (previous to the adoption of recommendations of "Scouting in the Lutheran Church") was due to local leadership and management.

4. The complaints that Scout leaders arrange hikes, camporees, and picnics on Sunday, thus preventing Lutheran boys from attending church, should be referred to the Scout leader, who must be informed that he must make changes in his calendar. A Lutheran troop under a Lutheran Scoutmaster would remove this difficulty.

5. The BSA makes no attempt to direct the religious or moral training of the boys in church troops. The Board quoted "Scouting Under Protestant Leadership":

> The Boy Scout councils, local and national, do not administer a Boy Scout troop anywhere. The parent institutions, churches, clubs, etc., administer their own troops. . . . The church leaders in the local communities should clearly understand that they have full charge of the administration of their own Scout troops through the supervision of the troop committee, which is appointed by the local church board or congregation. This troop committee secures the Scoutmaster and continues to serve as his supervisory committee.

We therefore reach these conclusions:

1. The Boy Scout organization is a secular institution with a secular program, whose spiritual motivation is to be provided by the sponsoring group. From official Scout manuals, and from official pronouncements, it appears to be evident that the Scout program can be classified as a club activity of a congregation included in the total religious education program of the congregation.

2. Membership in the Boy Scouts is not necessarily a denial of the faith nor necessarily unionistic. The BSA

does not intend to interfere with, or to weaken, the congregational program of youth training. Its avowed purpose is to offer a congregation its program of wider opportunity for the application of divine truths, a practical outlet for theoretical religious instruction, an opportunity for nature study, woodcraft, community service, and service to the church itself, always under the direct supervision and direction of the local church.

If the troop is a mixed troop, the matter becomes a problem in casuistry. But no Lutheran boy need to be penalized by asking to be excused from joint religious activity. The pastor of such a boy may require that all religious exercises or services be removed from the program of the local troop.

3. A congregationally controlled Scout troop derives the greatest benefits from the Scout program. The objectives of the Scout program in nature study, woodcraft, and social intercourse are not offensive but desirable. As a church we have nothing better to offer for that age group in that area of life. The Scout uniform does not make us responsible for the false religious views of others in the Scout movement.

The position of The Lutheran Church — Missouri Synod on Scouting is that it officially neither approves nor disapproves of this movement. The decision of the 1944 convention still represents our views on this problem: "The matter of Scouting should be left to the individual congregation to decide, and that under the circumstances Synod may consider her interests sufficiently protected."

## 2. Girl Scouts

Girl Scouts, Inc., organized by Mrs. Juliette Low in 1912, is an organization which aims "to bring to all girls the opportunity for group experience, outdoor life, and to learn through work, but more by play, to serve their community." Girls from 10 to 18 may join. Headquarters are in New York City. The organization has a program of hiking, camping, nature study, woodcraft, cooking, handicraft, etc.

Like boys in Scouting, the Girl Scouts has a pledge and law, uniforms and insignia, degrees of advancement, church troops and nonchurch troops, regular organization, and trained leaders. Although its method of organization and objectives are similar, the Boy Scouts and Girl Scouts are entirely independent of each other.

We may summarize our conclusions with the report of Synod's Board for Young People's Work in 1930 after making a thorough study of this movement:

1. The Pledge is not an oath.
2. The Law compels nothing contrary to the Word of God.
3. The "good turn" receives no objectionable emphasis.
4. The meetings do not open with a religious ceremony. No religious topics are discussed. On special occasions the meeting opens with a flag ceremony.
5. The supervision from headquarters is confined to prescribing uniform tests for advancement to higher grades. This supervision is necessary to preserve the standards.
6. The independence of every troop is safeguarded.
7. The unionistic tendencies, if they exist, are due to management and leadership of a local troop.

In our study we have discovered no reason for opposing the Girl Scouts.

The Board report concluded by suggesting that in view of these findings, wherever local conditions required, Girl Scout troops for Lutheran girls might be organized.

## Conclusion

Much more could have been written on these and other related organizations, but the limitations of space preclude. What has been presented will suffice to demonstrate that the problem of fraternalism, like all other evils of the world, will continue to plague the church as long as she remains the Church Militant. But the Gospel of Christ, which is *His* power in our lives and *our* chief weapon of defense and offense, assures us of the ultimate victory if we remain vigilant, diligent, and faithful as individuals and as a church.

# BIBLIOGRAPHY

Anderson, James. *The Constitutions of the Free Masons.* Printed by Wm. Hunter, 1723. (The original Book of Constitutions of the Grand Lodge)

Ball, J. Otis. *The Builder,* I, 287.

*The Builder.* A journal for the Masonic Student, published by the National Masonic Research Society, Anamosa, Iowa. $2.00. The editor is appointed under the authority of the Grand Lodge of Iowa.

"Busy Brotherly World of Freemasonry," *Life* (October 8, 1956). 14 pages.

Chase, *Digest of Masonic Law.*

*Citrus Mason and Eastern Star* Magazine (September 1933).

Clymer, *Ancient Mystical Oriental Masonry,* pp. 10, 11.

Coil, Dr. Elijah A. *The Relation of the Liberal Churches and the Fraternal Orders.*

Duncan, Malcolm C. *Masonic Ritual and Monitor.* Chicago, Ill.: Ezra A. Cook, 1947.

Gage, Asahel W. *The Builder,* I, 235.

Mackey Dr. Albert G. *Encyclopedia of Freemasonry,* II. New York, 1921. Pages 617, 619.

Mackey, Dr. Albert G. *Masonic Ritualist.* New York: Maynard-Merrill and Co. A Masonic monitor containing charges, general regulations, emblems, and accounts of the public ceremonies of the order.

Macoy, Robert. *Adoptive Rite Ritual.*

*Minnesota Proceedings.* 1896. Page 47.

*The New Age* Magazine. Published at Washington, D. C. (Official organ of the Supreme Council, 33d degree. AF and AM in U. S. A.).

Newton, Rev. J. Fort. *The Builders.* 7th ed., London, 1949.

*Proceedings of Grand Lodge of Texas.* Dec. 22, 1920. Page 22.

*Quarterly Bulletin of the Iowa Masonic Library.* Cedar Rapids, Iowa. An official publication of the Grand Lodge of Iowa.

*Quarterly Bulletin.* April, 1922. Page 3.

*Rituals of the Fraternal Order of Eagles.* Copyright 1949.

*Ritual of the Order of Eastern Star.* Washington, D. C., as amended, Sept. 1940.

*The Royal Arch Mason.* March 1957. Monthly periodical published by the General Grand Chapter, Royal Arch Masons.

*Square and Compass* Magazine. Nov. 15, 1925. Page 48.

Ward, J. S. M. *Freemasonry: Its Aims and Ideals.*

Webb, Thomas L. *The Freemason's Monitor.*

# PUBLISHERS AND REFERENCES

## I. Publishers

Boy Scouts of America, 2 Park Avenue, New York 16, N. Y.

The Charles T. Powner Company, P. O. Box 796, Chicago 90, Ill. (Publishers of rituals and other materials related to lodges)

Concordia Publishing House, 3558 S. Jefferson, St. Louis 18, Mo.

International Walther League, 875 N. Dearborn, Chicago, Ill.

Macoy Publishing and Masonic Supply Company, New York City, N. Y.

The Masonic History Company, Chicago, Ill. (Publishers of Mackey's *Encyclopedia of Freemasonry*)

The National Christian Association, 850 W. Madison St., Chicago, Ill. (Publishers of *Christian Cynosure,* a monthly. $1.50 a year)

## II. References

Box, Hubert S. *The Nature of Freemasonry.* London: Augustine Press, 1952.

Duncan, Malcolm C. *Masonic Ritual and Monitor.* Chicago: Ezra C. Cook, 1947.

Gould, R. F. *History of Freemasonry Throughout the World.* 6 vols. 1936.

Graebner, Theodore. *Handbook of Organizations.* St. Louis, Mo.: Concordia Publishing House, 1948.

Hannah, Walton. *Christian by Degrees.* London: Augustine Press, 1954.

Hannah, Walton. *Darkness Visible.* London: Augustine Press, 1952.

Mackey, Albert. *Encyclopedia of Freemasonry.* 3 vols. New York, N. Y.: Masonic History Co. Latest edition, 1946.

*The New Age.* 1735 Sixteenth St., N. W., Washington, D. C.: The Supreme Council 33, A. & A. Scottish Rite of Freemasonry. $1.50 a year. Appears monthly.

Pick and Knight. *The Pocket Manual of Freemasonry.* New York: Philosophical Library, 1953.

Pike, Albert. *Morals and Dogma.* 1871, but reprinted very often since that time.

*Statistics Fraternal Societies* (latest edition). The Fraternal Monitor, Powers Building, Rochester 14, N. Y.

Wilmhurst, W. L. *The Masonic Initiation.* London: John M. Watkins.